Understand, Manage, and Measure Cyber Risk

Practical Solutions for Creating a Sustainable Cyber Program

Second Edition

Ryan Leirvik

Apress®

Understand, Manage, and Measure Cyber Risk: Practical Solutions for Creating a Sustainable Cyber Program

Ryan Leirvik
Arlington, VA, USA

ISBN-13 (pbk): 978-1-4842-9318-8   ISBN-13 (electronic): 978-1-4842-9319-5
https://doi.org/10.1007/978-1-4842-9319-5

Managing Director, Apress Media LLC: Welmoed Spahr
Acquisitions Editor: Susan McDermott
Development Editor: Laura Berendson
Coordinating Editor: Jessica Vakili

Cover designed by eStudioCalamar

Distributed to the book trade worldwide by Springer Science+Business Media New York, 1 New York Plaza, New York, NY 10004. Phone 1-800-SPRINGER, fax (201) 348-4505, e-mail orders-ny@springer-sbm.com, or visit www.springeronline.com. Apress Media, LLC is a California LLC and the sole member (owner) is Springer Science + Business Media Finance Inc (SSBM Finance Inc). SSBM Finance Inc is a **Delaware** corporation.

For information on translations, please e-mail booktranslations@springernature.com; for reprint, paperback, or audio rights, please e-mail bookpermissions@springernature.com.

Apress titles may be purchased in bulk for academic, corporate, or promotional use. eBook versions and licenses are also available for most titles. For more information, reference our Print and eBook Bulk Sales web page at http://www.apress.com/bulk-sales.

Any source code or other supplementary material referenced by the author in this book is available to readers on the Github repository: https://github.com/Apress/Understand-Manage-and-Measure-Cyber-Risk. For more detailed information, please visit http://www.apress.com/source-code.

Printed on acid-free paper

Table of Contents

About the Author

Ryan Leirvik is a cybersecurity professional who has spent the better part of two decades enhancing information security programs at the world's largest institutions. With considerable US government and commercial sector experience, Ryan has employed his professional passion for cybersecurity at almost every level within an organization.

A frequent speaker on the topic of information security, Ryan fields questions such as "How do I make sure I have a sustainable cyber program?" This book was written to help answer that question.

Ryan is the founder and CEO of Neuvik. He has been the CEO of a cybersecurity research and development company, Chief of Staff and Associate Director of Cyber for the US Department of Defense, and a cybersecurity strategy consultant with McKinsey&Company. Ryan's technology career started at IBM. He has a master's degree in IT from Virginia Tech, an MBA from Case Western Reserve University, and a Bachelor of Science from Purdue University. Ryan is also on the faculty at IANS.

About the Technical Reviewer

Alex Esposito is an experienced cybersecurity consultant with a demonstrated history of working in management consulting specifically in the financial services, technology, and healthcare industries. She managed a team of technically backed business consultants to run advanced client delivery of Neuvik's cybersecurity solutions. She has vast security experience in business continuity, crisis management, disaster recovery, board-level reporting, CISO initiative prioritization, and risk framework implementation.

Acknowledgments

This book benefited considerably from the frequent consultation, discourse, and debate with Alex Esposito. Thank you for your time, participation, and sturdy contribution to this work.

Adam Nichols provided invaluable expertise. As always, thank you for your significant contributions to threat modeling, pushing beyond secure software, and your persistent demand for security confidence in all systems.

Also, Christophe Foulon—your interest, enthusiasm, and resolve were encouraging at just the appropriate times. Many thanks for your insights and overall enterprise security point of view.

Significant contributions were also made by Michael Mylrea, Rob Mauck, and Sounil Yu.

The team at Apress was an important part of launching this book. Thank you, Susan McDermott, for your kind reception and appreciation for the effort in compiling the material.

And, finally, Ava—your joyful spirit keeps me going every day.

Foreword 1

Some of us love building from scratch. As children, we gather stones and sticks and construct little cities where our imaginations can roam. As apparent grownups, we often must build something from scratch, except there is no such thing as "scratch." Everything has a history and a foundation—sometimes of neatly pointed stone, sometimes of toothpicks and chewing gum.

Tasked with building/rebuilding a security organization, we are confronted with a formidable challenge that feels like building from scratch; however, be assured that the bits and pieces are there—only strewn about in your organization.

After years as a scientist and research leader, my own security "from scratch" work ranged from building a product security organization and a privacy organization to twice creating world-class information security organizations within Fortune 500 corporations. There was never a truly blank sheet. The foundations were there but ranged from sticks and stones to a few solid pillars.

In my story, I was three years into my team's great work in creating the first Philips information security organization when I began to appreciate how much I enjoyed the build phase and not so much the operational phase. So, after a change in CIO, I retired from Philips to start my own consulting company. My brief sojourn into private practice ended when I joined Becton Dickinson (BD) to create another new CISO office—seeing a chance to build yet again and learn from a whole new set of mistakes. The new program at BD was firmly in place after four years, and I left to return to consulting, where I remain today.

Ryan Leirvik and I, for some time, have served as faculty at IANS Research (IANSResearch.com), a company providing its customers and the world with security insights from experienced practitioners. We did not meet there but were introduced by a colleague at McKinsey&Company and began a conversation about building InfoSec organizations. I quickly challenged Ryan to define *risk*. Although he looked a little startled, he did not hesitate to immediately provide a clear definition along with "By the way, I have just finished writing a book on building a strong security program that hinges on first defining risk." What followed was an exchange where each of us would make a statement or two about building a program and the other would pause, wide-eyed, and say, "Exactly!" It seems that I had found a kindred spirit—a builder who had worked with a wide variety of client CISOs on their programs, gaining a deep understanding of how a successful and sustainable program should be constructed. His cyber work at the US Department of Defense, his McKinsey consulting, and his advisory and survey work with IANS gave him a unique global view of our shared passion. My in-the-trenches build work with Fortune 500 multinationals and my CISO advisory work had given me a similar pragmatic perspective.

I was delighted to read Ryan's near-final copy of the book, and I jumped at the chance to provide this foreword. Ryan has assembled an extremely straightforward guide to building a strong risk-based cybersecurity program.

The world has significant problems with cybersecurity. We all appreciate the value provided by an ecosystem of pervasive, connected, smart things doing what we want and need. The problem is that while the complexity of hardware and software interconnection grows exponentially, so do the opportunities to exploit weaknesses. This can be quite rewarding for criminal and state actors seeking to illicitly profit or grow their power. On the cyber defense side, the complexity of what we must protect is astronomical. The landscape and its attack surface constantly grow, fold, and confound. This too often leads us to analysis (and solution) paralysis in addressing cybersecurity risk. Without due care, we can become reactive robots.

With an eye toward sustainable organizational success, Ryan begins his recipe with the development and propagation of shared definitions of *risk*, *threat*, *critical*, and other essential terms. This is the first of many step-by-step instructions on assembling the right elements, arranging them by priority, and establishing activities/projects to meet specific and measurable goals. Along the way, Ryan provides plenty of examples and small, simple rules, templates, and checklists to accelerate the first phases of the journey with emphasis on developing a short, meaningful list of targeted metrics. He provides a great way to start and grow your organization's risk management practice. Further, he emphasizes the takeaways by pointing out the pitfalls and providing meaningful examples of how a program might proceed.

I personally like to apply the Rumsfeldian lens to determine the completeness of a cybersecurity program, and this book hits all the marks. Ryan's book addresses the "known knowns" by systematically creating an asset inventory using a simple top-down practice. The "known unknowns" materialize as articulated risks assembled into a simple risk registry that is used to build consensus on the potential for harm, thus driving the priority of activities and projects. The problematic "unknown unknowns" are addressed by creating an information security organization that adopts a framework like the National Institute of Standards and Technology (NIST) CSF, preparing for the unexpected by using frameworks to ensure we have skills across all the cyber disciplines. Holistically, the book emphasizes the need for balance, and Ryan lays out a discipline of regular top-down reinspection to ensure the completeness of the program.

Not only does this book address the information security internals of creating and executing the plan, but it also emphasizes how the plan needs to engage the three levels of the larger organization: the board, management, and engineering. Ryan helps the CISO by considering what each level needs to do in the program and what the board member, manager, and engineer need to understand. His treatment of board reporting is particularly useful.

During my own journey to build security programs in the early days of the integrated IT enterprise, the road was often bumpy. This book enables a newly empowered CISO to proceed smoothly to construct a practical, connected, and accepted cybersecurity program where none existed before. It charts a clear path for the first two to four years of the program.

There are many other treatments more in depth and quantitative on aspects of cybersecurity and risk. They are easily folded in once the foundational cybersecurity program is up and running. This is the rare book that rapidly designs the first-version engine, builds it piece by piece (from near-scratch if necessary), gets it started, and brings the entire organization up to speed. You, the leader of a nascent cybersecurity program, can find herein a straightforward way to tackle cybersecurity complexity, organize the risks, and focus on the right problems and solutions in an ever-changing threat landscape. To you, the best of luck.

—Nicholas J. Mankovich, PhD

Foreword 2

They say that to understand someone, you ought to walk a mile in their shoes. As a leader of a corporate security program for a global Fortune 500 company with tens of thousands of employees, I think about this adage every time we engage with a contractor, auditor, or another third party. Consultants work with us to assess our capabilities, and they often have a mindset oriented toward "showing value." Inevitably though, our budget is tight, and so we can only engage for as short a time as possible.

These constraints usually mean that contractors do not have the time or scope to really walk in our shoes. Our complex operations might also mean that they need more than just a mile to really understand what we are up to. Out of a desire to help as best they can, consultants fall back to generic one-size-fits-all recommendations and security platitudes. Despite the good intent to show value, I frequently end up with something that looks pretty but lacks substance. Worst of all, some recommendations are merely distractions that would pull my team off higher priorities because the outside perspective lacked context.

This gap in understanding grows much larger when applied to a book full of advice about how to run a better program. Books are inherently generic, and it is entirely up to the reader to search for nuggets that may apply to their situation. Many books try to compensate for this by describing the Platonic ideal in great detail and as comprehensively as possible. Unfortunately, this may lead to unreadability and inapplicability because none of us lives in the ideal universe.

Companies, programs, and teams have a rhythm, like seasons. What was once fully mature and effective can decay over time and fall into disrepair. The people with a vision for an effective program find new companies, rotate to new positions, retire, or otherwise leave. As a result, even longstanding programs need to rebuild and rebirth what was working previously. Not to mention that the times (and risks) change and require us to adapt!

With this as a backdrop, I found myself at lunch with Ryan Leirvik, discussing risk, security, and everything, when Ryan pulled this book out of his bag and handed it to me. With gratitude but also some trepidation, I looked it over, wondering how useful it was really going to be and how much of a slog it would be to wade through (hopefully none of which showed up on my face).

It was a welcome surprise to find my fears were unfounded. What you have in your hand is a book that skillfully navigates around possible challenges of not understanding the nuances of your program and the obstacles you are trying to overcome. It is targeted at a specific audience, of course. However, if you are within the cybersecurity profession or even coming from a broader risk management perspective, I think that you will find this book worth your time.

So what lies ahead of you in the pages of this book? It is not the Platonic ideal of risk management—this book is not attempting to describe perfection. That said, it is also not a wild trip into the fringes of the topic. What lies ahead is clean practicality. I myself have worked before to define and create the perfect program and observed many others on the same hunt. I found a tendency to create something that looks good on paper—it often ends up academically airtight and full of lace and intricate detail as it tries to consider all the many what-if scenarios. Experience forced me to face the fact that my pursuit of perfection generally leads to something brittle and impractical when exposed to the rough treatment of the real world. I now prize flexibility and simplicity instead of attempting to have answers for everything and the rigidity that results.

This simplicity is what I find valuable within *Understand, Manage, and Measure Cyber Risk*. A fully realized risk management program has been sanded down and scrubbed of all the extras until what is left is clear, straightforward, and actually achievable. Will this book have all the answers? It will not. And that is the beauty of it! It contains core concepts and directional guidelines that allow you to adapt the content and dance with the needs of your unique organization. The holes in the guidance here are not actually things missing—they are windows, opened to let in the breeze.

The cover promises practical solutions for creating a sustainable cyber program. The fresh air and space between the core concepts are what deliver the practicality. A practical solution is almost always simple and achievable. Those qualities are what allow you to put it into practice. Ryan may not have walked a mile in your shoes, but he has done enough walking of his own to know what lies ahead for your journey. Rather than describe every step in excruciating detail, he offers the lay of the land and a map to help you navigate it. He also offers numerous stories and examples from his own travels that offer insight into how he and others traversed the same challenges that you may now be facing.

Ryan also managed to keep life in the book even as he delivers technical guidance on risk management. The straightforward language, with some light humor along the way, leads to a book that is accessible, interesting to read, and best of all useful. In the end, that moment over lunch when Ryan handed me a book turned out to be a moment of possibilities, not disappointment. I came away with what I value most in running a cybersecurity program—workable, relevant ideas shared with the flexibility to adapt them to my situation. Ryan distilled the concepts to their elemental ingredients so the book is a quick read, digestible by a busy professional. The book is as practical in form as it is in content.

Within my program, we use a down-and-dirty measurement to estimate the value of a thing—it is valuable if people use it. It does not matter how theoretically perfect your risk management program (in this case) may be; if people do not use your tools, process, and documentation, then it is not valuable. For me, Ryan's book meets the measurement. Not only did I read the whole book, which is not a foregone conclusion for this type of thing by any means, but I also keep returning to it to reference a passage or idea to see how I can apply it or be inspired. Perhaps this book can be your companion as well, helping you to meet—and dance with—your challenges.

—Tim Collyer

Introduction

When it comes to managing cybersecurity in an organization, many organizations tussle with some basic foundational components: understanding, managing, and measuring cybersecurity risk.

Without first understanding cybersecurity risk, many organizations struggle to effectively deploy and follow a risk-mitigating cybersecurity program. The supporting functions of program management and effectiveness measurement begin to fail, as the risk is simply not well understood across the key areas of management, technology, and executive oversight. Programs lacking a sharply articulated view of risk lose out on the benefits an objective-based program provides, for example, a long-term view of risk, a view of the current risk tolerance, gaps in program controls that introduce known and unknown risks, and measures that are appropriate for the board of directors.

One simple way to identify if your organization falls into the "cyber risk tussle" category is to raise three very basic but fundamental questions: (1) Is the head of your organization able to articulate cybersecurity risk in one to two sentences? (2) Are key executives/managers in your organization able to provide a similar, short-but-on-point answer to this same question? (3) Could each person in the organization provide a clear answer to what "cybersecurity" means to their role, including engineers, front-line employees, contract specialists, recruiters, and sales team members?

If the answer is no, you are not alone. And this book is for you.

This book is a practitioner's guide to laying down foundational components of an effective cybersecurity risk management program for organizational management, technology, and executive oversight, ultimately keeping up with the business and reducing business risk. Recent examples of organizational challenges are provided for practical context, and pitfalls to avoid are offered as controls.

Overall, this book provides an easy-to-follow categorical approach to identifying what is "at risk," applying a suitable approach to managing that risk, and getting started on simple-but-effective measures on program effectiveness at both the strategic (board) and tactical (management and technology) levels.

To date, a plethora of cybersecurity management advice has been delivered to the public—many with sound advice, management approaches, and technical solutions. Few have offered a common 1-2-3 theme to help pull it all together. This book attempts to do just that.

PART I

The Problem

Keep in Mind

To best understand the cybersecurity problem, keep three concepts in mind:

- Technology is an enabler.

- Imperfect humans build technology.

- Advantageous actors misuse technology to reap rewards.

CHAPTER 1

What Is the Problem?

Introduction

The information technology we rely upon is a tremendous enabler and also… imperfect. Unplanned exceptions and incidental impairments exist in the underlying and interconnected technology, deviating its actual functionality away from the ideal. These imperfections expose attractive perforations perfectly accommodating for an unintended user. This is the problem of cybersecurity.

It all starts at the beginning: the decision to use and deploy Internet-connected technology.

Organizations generally select, deploy, and use information technology[1] (IT) as an enabler. Preceding all other miraculous qualities, IT enables practical communication and commerce through the increased efficiency and improved effectiveness of almost every common business process (e.g., sales, finance, communications, human resources, inventory management). Programmable systems, software, and networks offer the possibility to work together—processing and sharing information—to provide organizations the means to meet certain goals and objectives.

---

[1] For the purposes of this discussion, information technology is used to mean the interoperable and connected technology that is involved in the development, maintenance, and use of computer systems, software, and networks that process, store, or transmit data. (Note "data." For both information security and information technology, the distinction between "data" and "information" is important.)

Corporations, governments, partnerships, educational institutions, charities, cooperatives, as well as both not-for-profit and nongovernmental organizations all rely on IT at some level. Even pure-play FORTUNE[2] Global 500 technology companies, whose organizational goals are directly related to the development and use of technology, rely heavily on technology's interconnectedness and data-sharing as an enabling function within the organization itself.

The trouble is… technology is flawed.[3]

The flaws in information technology are not exactly the fault of the underlying technology itself. Humans create technology, and humans, for all our achievements, are imperfect.[4] So, perhaps, for this discussion about information security, a simple understanding that humans are not perfect is a sufficient baseline for the fact that the underlying technology, which humans create, is also imperfect.

These technology imperfections have names. For instance, a development oversight may be an error (or "bug"[5]) in deployed software, a misstep (or "misconfiguration") in a network configuration, a deficiency

---

[2] FORTUNE is a trademark of Fortune Media IP Limited, registered in the United States and other countries.

[3] For all of those in the technology community working tirelessly to bring out the best of what is possible and also for those in the legal community working to clarify definitions for the protection of clients, the word *flaw* (and each derivative) is used to imply imperfection as it relates to the pursuit of perfection. This word is not, in any way, used to imply defective, broken, or damaged as it relates to any technology's intended use.

[4] Humanity's potential and expressed capability to be perfect is a subject ripe for deep exploration and discussion; however, realizing the full human potential is not the focus of this particular information security discussion.

[5] The word *bug* is a widely adopted term to describe a defect or malfunction. One first-use story is Grace Hopper's finding a moth in the Harvard Mark II (a.k.a. Aiken Relay Calculator). She removed the moth, jammed in the mechanical relay causing an error, and taped it inside a log book.

(or "unplanned exception") in a supported hardware device, or simply an accepted risk in the way it was designed.[6]

Furthermore, these imperfections are either known or unknown by system administrators at any given time. They may reside in either convenient places (i.e., easily identifiable and easily fixed with low impact to operations) or inconvenient places (i.e., not easily identifiable and operationally hard to fix). They may be intentional (i.e., purposely designed to create an alternative interaction) or unintentional (i.e., not purposely designed). They may be small in size or very large in both size *and* scale.

These inherent imperfections represent an important aspect when it comes to organizational reliability on the technology used to meet certain objectives: susceptibility for unintended interaction and functionality[7] just waiting to be discovered. For instance, an unplanned exception in a deployed system can provide a "way in" for an unauthorized user, or an "outsider," to gain unauthorized-but-available access to the "inside" of a system or an organization.[8]

The problem these imperfections create, however, is not just a simple functionality impairment needing a software patch or hardware fix once discovered; users can be quite annoyed when technology does not function the way it should. But rather, it's the exposure of an attractive perforation in the technology itself that is perfectly accommodating for an unintended user to interact with it in unplanned ways. Introduce data,

---

[6] From a security design point of view, much of the underlying technology of the Internet itself was built on trust. This is not exactly a design flaw or an oversight, but rather an interaction consideration in design that would be hard to predict, an "intentional use" point worth considering when debating the security aspects of deployed technology.

[7] Susceptibility for *failure* is not addressed for the purposes of this discussion. (See the preceding *flaw*.)

[8] Leaving for a moment alternative access pathways available to insiders, such as the insider motivated to wreak havoc on an organization or a socially engineered employee unwittingly providing secrets to an outsider.

communication, and operational functionality that requires safeguarding, and that possible "way" into that technology becomes much more attractive to an outsider. This is the problem of information security, or cybersecurity.[9]

---

[9] Several definitions exist for cybersecurity. The US government formally defines cybersecurity as the "Prevention of damage to, protection of, and restoration of computers, electronic communications systems, electronic communications services, wire communication, and electronic communication, including information contained therein, to ensure its availability, integrity, authentication, confidentiality, and nonrepudiation." The White House, Cybersecurity Policy, National Security Presidential Directive (NSPD)-54/Homeland Security Presidential Directive (HSPD)-23.

CHAPTER 2

Why Is It Complicated?

Introduction

ABSTRACT

Technology's imperfections are where the cybersecurity problem *begins*, exposing attractive perforations in its intended functionality. Deploy imperfect technology imperfectly, and these unintended perforations multiply in innumerable ways. Layer imperfect technologies into existing technologies, each with perpetual pursuits to communicate and interact with interoperable counterparts, and these perforations spread in orthogonally interconnected and largely unmanageable ways, introducing vulnerabilities either visible or perfectly hidden for the malicious individual, or group, to exploit. This is the complication of the cybersecurity problem.

Appreciating the fact that technology is inherently imperfect opens the aperture for a wider view into the real complication of cybersecurity: inherently flawed technology is everywhere. Critical assets and business functions rely on this technology, and somewhere there is a security team, with a chief information security officer (CISO) in command, uncovering the security challenges to protect others against its misuse.

R. Leirvik, *Understand, Manage, and Measure Cyber Risk*,
https://doi.org/10.1007/978-1-4842-9319-5_2

Technology Is Everywhere

Technology is as pervasive in modern organizations as it is in modern life. Some sort of computer system or sensor exists in many commercial, industrial, and consumer products today. Consumer vehicles today can have a tremendous volume of sensors that create over 2,000 signals from various electronic control units at any given time.[1] Farming equipment can contain an uncountable number of embedded computing sensors to monitor crops, livestock activity,[2] and available resources. Almost no adult living in a first-world country leaves the house[3] without at least one computing technology device.

But technology's pervasiveness is simply the boundary of the problem's complication. That is, the simple fact that technology is becoming nearly ubiquitous speaks to where the technology is located (i.e., the physical location of deployed technology). The real problem in cybersecurity is not so much that the technology itself is flawed and that it is nearly everywhere, but rather, technology is flawed, it is everywhere, and it is increasingly becoming more and more complex.

---

[1] *Popular Mechanics*, Ben Wojdyla, "How it Works: The Computer Inside Your Car," www.popularmechanics.com/cars/how-to/a7386/how-it-works-the-computer-inside-your-car/, February 21, 2012.

[2] Yes, "attaching a sensor and tracking device to a cow will give a farmer the ability to track the cow's activity level, health, and other key behaviors." *AgriTech Tomorrow*, Len Calderone, "Smart Sensors in Farming," www.agritechtomorrow.com/article/2019/02/smart-sensors-in-farming/11247, December 26, 2019.

[3] Admit it. Although a refreshing feeling occasionally, leaving a dwelling without some sort of IT device is not a normal activity (especially for a reader of a book on information security). However, you may think about what that device connects to a bit differently after completing this book.

Technology Is Complex

Technology's ever-evolving complexity exacerbates the cybersecurity problem in orthogonal ways. Not only is technology heavily relied upon, but it's also constantly changing and self-adapting. While changing and adapting to various environments, this persistently changing technological construct is also in perpetual pursuit to communicate and connect with interoperable counterparts (e.g., devices, sensors, networks, other computing systems).

The Internet of Things (commonly referred to as *IoT*) represents this phenomenon. Devices that are not functionally required to provide connected information delivery are communicating in ways that increase their overall complexity: for example, a fashionable fall prevention smart belt that comes with sensors to monitor and alert the belt wearer.[4] And sometimes, this information connectivity works in ways that may directly counter the device's intended function, like the Internet-connected personal safe[5] or the human exercise location tracker.[6] As manufacturers are addressing the demand for convenient and relevant information, the IoT interconnectedness brings about risks in unintended ways: pathways to the device and a surface area to other networked devices on the same network or in the same connected ecosphere.

---

[4] Also, the less fashionable but more functional Helite Hip'Air protective belt.

[5] OK, quick risk check. This is a book on identifying and reducing cyber risk. At this point, this concept should raise more than one risk indicator: a consumer safe, designed to protect critical physical assets (e.g., money, jewels, sensitive documents) and offered to a consumer who typically has limited understanding of embedded technology is discoverable by, and connected to, the outside world riddled with attackers looking for exactly these types of valuables.

[6] Uncomfortable subject for certain but also worth considering is the unintended technology use. Here immediate GPS-based social media postings of exercise locations exposed military complexes and put exercisers at risk of stalkers.

Even hardware that used to be "hard" is now soft. Networking from switches and cables has become virtual, as software-defined "everything" has taken hold.[7]

This complexity makes defending technology very difficult. As the complexity of technology deployments increases, securing the systems becomes even more difficult, even when manufacturers focus heavily on cybersecurity risk mitigation. Take, for example, Apple Inc.'s[8] products that are developed in a completely closed system. The company single-handedly defines and builds its own technology within a closed ecosystem.[9] This is the type of supply chain management and fulfillment orchestration that makes many technology companies exceedingly envious. And yet, security researchers[10] can find flaws in almost every single build.

Technology Was Built on Trust

The underlying design and networking that make software and hardware function properly were not built with malicious use as the paramount risk to address. Computing design and telecommunication networking were expensive in the late 1960s, so building additional functionality to consider and address perceived abuse would have driven up costs. Not to mention that communication between parties was initially trusted—one could argue that those using it, more than 25 years before it was commercially

---

[7] For example, infrastructure as code, where certain infrastructure needs may be virtualized quickly rather than configuring and deploying physical hardware.

[8] Likely needing no introduction, Apple Inc. is the multinational consumer electronics, computer software, and computer services company that brought you, individual business person, the Lisa well before its time back in 1983.

[9] This includes a seamless and cross-functionally controlled supply chain.

[10] A kind euphemism for hackers, criminals, and others is used here out of respect for everyone in this field.

available, were already trusted. For example, today's Internet Protocol suite was originally designed to transmit data to and from *known* parties, typically engineers who knew each other. When information was sent, a phone call between known engineers could confirm the message's proper arrival to that known person. Later, Transmission Control Protocol was added to provide some sort of verification that the data was or was not received, so that engineers did not have to call each other, or wait for a reply, to know that the message was received.

Fast-forward to today's use of that same networking technology and transfer of data, and that trust no longer exists. This lack of trust is a key driver of the need to design and deploy security controls *before* the technology is deployed and used. The challenge here is that not all technologies are designed with security as a design parameter before they are released for use, thus compounding the cybersecurity problem by every released technology that does not consider its misuse prior to that release, continuing to create less-than-resistant ways for attackers to achieve malicious objectives.

Technology Is an Opportunity for Misuse

Untrustworthy or malicious groups and individuals exist in the world. Seeking to do harm to others or achieve some sort of gainful advantage, malicious characters and groups typically use the least resistant ("easiest") means to reach a desired objective.

Before the interconnectedness of computers and devices, malevolent intentions by individuals had to be carried out in person or contain some sort of physical[11] element. Today, however, direct connections to valuable targets exist through deployed technology, making it easier to reach

---

[11] The word *physical* means relative to the human body. Arguably electric transmission and computing is physical; however, in this context it refers to the proximity to the person (i.e., the target).

targets. These connections almost eliminate the need to be physically close to any prey or victim, uncomplicating the effort to camouflage, or physically hide, an offensive strike.

Designs of technology used in IT that do not include a security element against such threats face substantial challenges when exposed to would-be attackers. The continual good-vs.-evil use cases of artificial intelligence demonstrated through machine learning illustrate these challenges.

The Fundamental Risk Is Not Always Understood

Almost all the technologies used in organizations are imperfect in some way, and decisions are required to address the maintenance and use of these technologies. These decisions can either worsen or improve the imperfections, making it easier or harder for malicious attackers to exploit these imperfections to their advantage. As the technology persistently morphs to meet the demands of business and consumers, layers of interconnected technology and the management of that technology swell. Even highly distinguished commercial technology providers are not immune to unintended exceptions in deployed technologies, based on either the technology itself or a management decision regarding the technology. But this is not the fundamental risk, per se. The risk is how such unintended use of the technology *impacts* the organization. Yet, many organizations lack a risk model that appropriately considers the overall impact to the organization or business. If these concepts remain uncorrected, it may be fair to say that deploying inherently flawed technology in an organization carries with it a *business risk* that likely is not well understood at any given time.

Now try explaining that to an executive.

... and Business Leaders Need to Know What to Do

The fundamental challenge businesses face while relying on technology is the ability to understand the unintended risks to the business with its use. Many in the information technology field with backgrounds in technology's misuse understand this. However, business leaders, without deep backgrounds in technology or its misuse, may not inherently understand this. These business leaders are the ones who need a quick way to understand the risk and accurately determine the value in addressing it, relative to the business. Since technology, as an enabler, must keep up with the business, fixing it must too. And astute business leaders ask astute questions to understand and address these risks, such as the following:

- How much is it worth to fix a vulnerability?

- What is the value, or utility, of our overall security investment?

- How much should the organization invest in security going forward?

- How might the organization measure real effectiveness?

- How much would an adversary have to spend to gain access to our sensitive assets?

- How much do we need to spend to slow down an adversary?

All good questions. But without a clear understanding of the intersection of technology and business, the ability to identify and communicate the actual risk will simply not exist.

From a technology point of view, perpetual visibility into deployed technology and how that technology is owned and operated within the organization is the starting point for addressing this problem. From a business point of view, the ability to understand the actual risk, as it relates to the business, is the perpetual risk decision-making end goal for addressing this problem. In between these two points of view is the ability to determine a mitigation value so that informed decisions may be made by business leaders who need to know what to do. Determining *value* is not easy, but it may be simplified with a common way to view and communicate cyber risk, as a common approach provides for a standard from which a "risk line" or "risk tolerance" threshold could be determined, agreed to, and used for the business.

Flatly explaining to an executive that deployed technology has security imperfections and that underlying procedures and controls must be put in place to compensate for these imperfections (both known and unknown) invites the executive to probe or even challenge the statement from any angle. This approach could quickly lead everyone down a scattered path trying to figure out which imperfection to track and how much to invest in mitigating it. The utility of this approach soon becomes marginal, and everyone becomes frustrated. The lack of a common cybersecurity risk language, the inability to provide clear answers to the executive board based on a common view of risk, and no clear organizational mission alignment are missing in this approach. Unfortunately, this is relatively common when explaining cybersecurity risk mitigation to all types of very smart and nimble-minded business leaders.

Keep in Mind

The following approaches complicate the understanding of risk in any organization:

- Lack of a common cybersecurity risk language

- Unclear answers for proper oversight

- Oh, and... umm... distractors

Three weighty complications typically exist when trying to understand cybersecurity risk in any one organization: (1) a lack of a common cybersecurity risk language, (2) unclear answers for proper oversight, and... oh, umm... (3) distractors. Each complication deserves deeper consideration.

Lack of a Common Cybersecurity Risk Language

IT was widely introduced in commercial organizations in 1994.[12] And yet, a quarter century later, managers, engineers, and board members still speak different languages when it comes to technology and management. This language divide creates a disconnect in the strategy-to-management-to-operational connection that is critical to overall organizational risk management, not to mention overall business management.

Now enter the challenge of securing IT. A clear strategy-to-management-to-operational link is critical in effective cybersecurity risk management. The absence of such a link complicates the ability for the three functions (i.e., strategic planning, managerial execution, and operational controls/engineering) to align on one common language, or model, for managing cyber risk. For example, boards oversee cybersecurity risk as part of the organizational risk, managers typically view cybersecurity as a risk that needs to be managed just like any other risk in the organization, and engineers almost always view cybersecurity as a technical imperfection that needs to be corrected.

---

[12] Seeing as this is neither a book about the Internet nor a historical account of information technology, the launch of Netscape Navigator in 1994 will serve as a relative point of time when Internet technology, as part of the broader information technology, became widely available for commercial use. It also serves as a convenient example of cybersecurity, as convenience (e.g., online accessibility) tussled with the need for security protocols (e.g., secure financial transactions).

The three organizational levels often struggle to collectively articulate the actual risk. However, the real struggle, or challenge, surfaces when the three come together in an effort to properly manage and measure risk mitigation through data within the organization (the intersection of technology and business).

Managers looking to satisfy board requests are challenged in aligning insightful risk management to appropriate controls coverage. With several risk management models and frameworks from which to choose, actual risk management pitfalls exist when a chosen model or framework does not properly fit the risk, causing many to over-index one area (e.g., tooling) while missing another critical area entirely (e.g., incident response). For example, one might choose a controls-based framework as a risk management guide and focus too much on specific technology or IT governance while simultaneously missing an overall management model—losing the ability to educate executives *and* the board on how overall risk is being reduced. Alternatively, one might focus too much on a security management requirements framework and miss the ability to communicate the business value of programs through impact-articulating risk models and insightful measures. And yet another might rely too much on a home-grown technical risk approach and completely miss the ability to meet regulators' demands through an understood translation table for what the company is actually doing to meet what regulators require.

Both executive and managerial alignment throughout the organization is essential for clear security reporting and structure—from the board to each business unit—and making the alignment for these two is one common language. Don't believe it? Try to go to a board without one consistent and common way of defining how risk is being managed within the organization. This approach may raise more questions ripe for unclear answers rather than an approach that establishes a basis for insightful responses.

Unclear Answers for Proper Oversight

In addition to executives that need to know what to do for proper management direction, board members need to know what is being done for proper oversight. To that end, board members commonly have clear questions when it comes to cybersecurity. Many questions have clear objectives, such as the following:

- How do we leverage metrics to tell an effective story, driving investment decisions?

- What mechanisms or tools are in use to appropriately qualify, or even quantify, risk?

- What examples would help point us in the right direction?

The impact of a cyber incident can vary by organization, and with that variation, so does the relative cybersecurity risk. Operational impacts, reputational impacts, legal impacts, and even licensing impacts are typically different between organizations, as they are highly dependent on the type of business, governance of data/systems, and severity of a cybersecurity incident.[13]

Many organizations speak about technical tools, controls, fixes, and expert people to address this risk. While greatly important, these are tactical solutions, as they solve particular risk management problems like detection, monitoring, blocking, and remediation. These solutions, however, do not solve the strategic oversight problems that are the concerns of directors or even potential investors.

---

[13] Exact definitions of the words *incident* and *event* are not quite standardized for all cyber circumstances across all business and government activities. Current policies, laws, and regulations do define these terms within their respective areas.

The problem directors have to solve, from an overnight perspective, is more strategic: the overall organizational cyber maturity relative to the risk. In other words, does the organization have a grip on its real risk, and, if so, what is the state of its maturity in managing that risk? This leads everyone back to the beginning: what questions do we need to ask to get a sense of the real cybersecurity risk within the organization? In essence, where do we start?

Oh, and Umm... Distractors

If there is one constant in cybersecurity, it may be the ever-changing kaleidoscope of terms, expressions, and phrases around newsworthy exploitation events and the solutions developed to address them. The flurry of new descriptors around tactics, techniques, and procedures that drive interest and demand for new tools and methodologies to address previously undiscovered threats or vulnerabilities can leave any executive or manager scurrying around for context. The challenge is putting the terms, events, mitigations, and solutions into context... quickly.

Want to test this? Simply raise questions during any of the next meetings. What's the best cloud-based intrusion detection solution? What's the best solution for QR code scams? What's the cover term for the group that targeted the power plant last week? When are we planning the next Purple Team real-time assessment and training session for our incident responders? What critical findings did our detection engineering team discover?

Each categorically discrete and distinct item may be legitimate within a security department or at the managerial level; however, the danger of organizational distraction shows up quickly with executives when there is no authoritative, or common, structure to lean on for which to internally categorize a new "thing."

Distractors in cybersecurity, as with any professional discipline, pose real challenges to operational efficiency. One real challenge is the "newest widget" distractor, which is the latest technology solution enticing the security-inquisitive toward the "chase the shiny object" black hole, pulling critical attention deep into the tactical singularity that the technology provides and far, far away from the operational business galaxy.

Challenges like these sometimes result in a panicked mania when trying to come back to, or align with, the gravitational necessity of a sufficient risk management plan. These distractors pull managers and executives far away from the actual risk problem and more toward a discrete technical solution. What suffers in the meantime is the ability to focus on the overall risk problem in order to solve for broader program solutions, for example, how to develop an informed view of critical gaps in current controls relative to the business or how to gain insights into addressing enterprise goals and measures or how to identify impractical legacy tools.

Without a sharp focus on a clear and encompassing set of cybersecurity categories found in an enterprise risk program, distractions can cause real harm. Some distractors, in the form of new technologies, can actually increase the risk by adding to an organization's *attack surface*.[14]

As flawed and complex technology continues to be woven into the fabric of everyday modern life, attention to the crucial operational link between strategic risk oversight and tactical risk mitigation is imperative.

---

[14] Definitions of "attack surface" vary. In essence, "attack surface" includes the external-facing organizational information technology, in its entirety, that is susceptible to intrusion.

CHAPTER 3

How to Address This Problem

Introduction

ABSTRACT

Connected to, and contained within, imperfect technology are assets organizations deem as critical... and attackers find valuable. The ability to clearly identify and describe this observation in meaningful ways is a critical step to addressing the cybersecurity problem—so that it may be managed as a *risk*. With the risk actually understood, organizational functions may become clearer, and appropriate measures of effectiveness become more insightful.

As imperfect technology permeates the fabric of everyday enterprise and personal life, security risks introduced by technology imperfections continue to rise. Unfortunately, enterprise security risk management requires rapid response and persistent monitoring to identify and remediate imperfections (e.g., *flaws, vulnerabilities, deployment missteps*) relevant to the organization's ability to protect critical assets and business functions. Achieving an overall enterprise cybersecurity program is a multistep process that leaves many managers and organizations uncertain about where to begin.

Here, perhaps, the best place to start is the beginning: understanding the risk that needs to be mitigated.

© Ryan Leirvik 2023
R. Leirvik, *Understand, Manage, and Measure Cyber Risk,*
https://doi.org/10.1007/978-1-4842-9319-5_3

Understand the Risk

In one sentence, what is an organization's cybersecurity risk?

(Pause to think.)

It's not an easy question to answer, right? Certainly not easy to answer in a crisp sentence without a considerable understanding of, or insight into, the core problem.

After consideration, most answers take the shape of a *cybersecurity event*,[1] a *computer hack*, or a *breach*—something that sounds horrific and denotes hurt put upon a victim (a person or an organization) in any number of ways. This type of quick answer is naturally echoed by many sources—public media sources, private individuals, and sometimes business leaders—far away from the day-to-day core problem. But this makes sense: mostly all humans seek immediate answers to uncertain or ambiguous phenomena.[2] Therefore, a quick, imperfect description such as a *hack* or a cybersecurity *breach* is fine; it's typically not wrong, per se. However, it does not answer the risk question. What is it about the *hack* or the *breach* that introduced a risk?

Answering the risk question is typically where things get a bit scattered. Answers sometimes revolve around cybersecurity program failures, the attackers' motivations, some nation-state sponsorship, or lack of talented resources to combat the hacks. All of these may be decent and honorable

---

[1] The term cybersecurity *event* is used rather than cybersecurity *incident*, as many organizations are required to establish a clear and intentional distinction between an incident and an event for a host of appropriate reasons. (See the section "Know the Applicable Laws and Regulations.")

[2] Pause for a moment here. You're in the right place for a book on cybersecurity if you notice a pesky curiosity to clearly define the obscure. If not, keep reading. At the end of the book, you should have a visceral reaction to quick answers saddled with uniformed assumptions. One could argue that true cybersecurity demands an exploration into the depths of uncertainty and ambiguity, searching for a way to provide a compendious answer to the unknown. Afterall, it's within the unexamined assumption where the attacker flourishes.

answers for the inability to detect or manage the event, but they are not sufficient answers to address, communicate the understanding of, or align with the actual risk.

Answers that address the actual risk provide insights into the *impact* the organization experienced, such as the loss of, or tampering with, certain organizational assets (as in data, devices, applications, networks, and users[3]). Assets are the target for malicious activities. Activities against critical assets (if stolen, terminated, or changed by an unauthorized actor) can significantly harm vital operations and/or the financial well-being of an organization.[4] The organizational impact due to data forfeiture or operational deprivation of critical assets (for which the organization must provide due care) is the real risk. Therefore, a clear distinction between the assets affected by unauthorized users and the event that resulted from the unauthorized activity is very important for understanding the actual risk.

Organizational assets, like data or certain systems, affected during a cybersecurity event that led directly to a work stoppage or imposed a significant cost to the organization are part of what is referred to as *critical assets*; these are *at risk*. The trouble for most organizations is that what is critical, or the business impact of lost or manipulated data or other assets, is not always well known *before* the event. Organizations often learn what assets are targets (a.k.a. items of interest) for outside attackers through "lessons learned" after the first cybersecurity event. This what-should-have-been-protected learning moment can be a very expensive and embarrassing lesson on both organizational cost and impact. At times, this may become the moment when leadership attention quickly turns inward to understanding and mitigating the real risk.[5]

---

[3] See the section "Inventory and Categorize Critical Assets."

[4] The terms *confidentiality*, *integrity*, and *availability* (a.k.a. the CIA triad), as they relate to impact, are addressed later.

[5] In some cases, these lessons and management actions are learned in real time, a less-than-effective way to learn about what is at risk while simultaneously mitigating the risks.

Being clear about the real risk means identifying the key critical data and systems (i.e., critical assets) that endanger organizational sustainability or threaten the organization's core business functions.[6] This means having a sharp understanding of the risk through categorizing the critical assets and determining the causes/consequences/accountability of an incident.[7]

But identifying critical assets to understand the real risk is not easy. The fundamental basis of knowing critical systems means that an organization has identified all technology assets—a typically undesirable struggle many do not fully tackle. Identifying and developing risk-mitigating protections must hinge on the assets themselves, not the other way around. Developing risk mitigations before understanding the risk shifts attention to solutions before the problem is even well defined. This is the reason identifying the actual risk through critical assets is so imperative. Tackling the view into all assets, including third parties and the technology supply chain, turns the attention to the actual organizational assets at risk. Once these assets are defined, defensive controls and established triggers have a known role to play. Then and only then can the checks on controls effectiveness truly be measured.

---

[6] This is information security. US Code Title 44 defines information security as "The protection of information and information systems from unauthorized access, use, disclosure, disruption, modification, or destruction in order to provide confidentiality, integrity, and availability."

[7] Now enter a cybersecurity incident—something that raises to the level of realized risk and achieves recognition status with executives. As the NIST SP 800-160 Vol. 2 defines a cyber incident, "[a]ctions taken through the use of an information system or network that result in an actual or potentially adverse effect on an information system, network, and/or the information residing therein."

Manage the Risk

Simplifying how risk is managed is no easy task in any organization. A few rules, however, are worthy of immediate establishment in the absence of a cybersecurity program:

- Apply a framework (i.e., a structural frame for proper management).

- Structure the organization (i.e., the staff and reporting for proper management).

- Set a review frequency (i.e., a cadence for program progress).

- Prepare to respond (and recover).

Apply a Framework

Cybersecurity risk management frameworks abound, and no one framework applies perfectly to any one organization. However, an established framework provides a single integrated approach to addressing the cybersecurity risk problem. Employing one helps shape the organizational thinking and the overall enterprise technique around common areas of cybersecurity risks from a top-down point of view. Sounds simple? Conceptually, it is. But identifying and sticking with the "right" top-down, structured framework is not only challenging for the typically bottom-up security practitioner; it's also a key source of confusion and frustration when mapping activities into structured categories.

The structure of a framework, however, is the indispensable component of a defendable cybersecurity risk program. Applying a known cybersecurity risk management framework—especially in the absence of one—immediately brings shape to a security practice around common objective-based disciplines in any organization, regardless of industry. In many organizations, applying a framework is a fundamental first step in organizing the cybersecurity practice for or within the enterprise.

When applying a framework, one area of immediate value is the categorical range of items provided that typically go overlooked or ignored—for example, incident response preparedness. When choosing and applying the NIST CSF,[8] for instance, the Framework Core guides the implementer to desired activities that include the broad functions for a management program. In a world where many practitioners can become easily distracted with the more gripping activities in Protect and Detect (e.g., defending in real time, new tooling), applying the NIST CSF forces attention on less immediately gripping but as (if not more) important activities like an organization's ability to respond to, and recover from, an incident. This is immediately valuable, as questions begin to rise around the existence, and possible testing, of incident response plans—that is, preparing for the inevitable. Why is this valuable? It encourages an organizational focus on prompt incident response.

Applying a framework as a first step offers a perspective on how to best understand the risk, at least broadly, and appropriately plan for the realization of risk. The trouble is that cybersecurity frameworks come in different shapes and sizes, as they each address risks at various levels of the organization. For example, program frameworks address the overall state of a cybersecurity program, control frameworks address appropriate functional controls for security assurance, and general risk frameworks address overall risk. Specific frameworks are covered in Chapter 5, but the first step is to choose one and apply it.

---

[8] The National Institute of Standards and Technology (NIST) released the first version (1.0) of the Framework for Improving Critical Infrastructure Cybersecurity (CSF) on February 12, 2014. This framework acts as a structured way to help understand and address cybersecurity risks faced by any organization, not just critical infrastructure.

Structure the Organization

With this first step in place, practitioners have a guide to assign associated staff in an organized, risk-informed manner, based on the pursuit of certain activities. The selected framework to apply can help provide the conceptual shape, or structure, for foundational activities, or areas, to be managed. This means that organizational positions, roles, and responsibilities may be informed by key, foundational activities found in the framework to ensure proper coverage in practice.

Many organizations struggle with just how to shape their cybersecurity organizations. Following a known framework can help. If set appropriately, strategic questions about how much to invest in security and how to best mitigate risks can have informed answers, paving the way to understanding and measuring value (or utility) of risk mitigation investments: that is, the value (or utility) of the investment made in cybersecurity. (Organizational structure is covered in Chapter 5.)

Set a Review Frequency

An operational program should not remain static. With a cybersecurity framework and an organizational structure in place, a planned review of current progress toward assigned due dates helps answer a common question: *how are we doing*? A standard review of the activities set by the organization (based on key activities) can help with the frequent challenge of cybersecurity activity prioritization. (Chapter 5 provides an overview of program review elements.)

Prepare to Respond (and Recover)

The clock is ticking the second someone notices an event that becomes an incident. Every second the incident goes unhandled, the organizational impact is exacerbated, raising potentially greater damages and costs to the organization. Since incident response is often a less-observed practice than buying new tools and hiring new staff, the activity becomes a key area of focus for actual risk management. (Key considerations are covered in Chapter 5.)

Measure the Impact of Risk Management

What an organization measures in cybersecurity indicates the level at which they view the security problem. The ability to quantify uncertainty in a way that provides decision-makers the appropriate level of risk mitigation and coverage through measurement is necessary to answer the question: how are we doing?

As with any enterprise program, a proper feedback mechanism is critical for measuring performance. Cybersecurity management is no different. And just like any other program, exactly *what* and *how* to measure depends deeply on the level of risk understanding.

Keep in Mind

To best address proper feedback, keep the following in mind:

- Choose risk-informative measures.

- Apply appropriate resources.

- Drive for value.

- Be clear on what to measure.

- Avoid chasing perfect (it's not that valuable).

Choose Risk-Informative Measures

Choosing a risk-informative set of measures begins with understanding the risk. A well-understood risk may be articulated, and a well-articulated risk may be decomposed into key components for measuring. These components become the fundamentals for key performance indicators (KPIs), key risk indicators (KRIs), objectives and key results (OKRs), and simple measures (more on this in Chapter 7).

Organizations struggle with what to measure, what data is available to inform the measures, and which outcomes to achieve. It can all be very hard to tackle up front, and many organizations try to measure everything possible. A few pitfalls exist with a "tackle everything" approach. Tackling everything up front without a clear risk objective can (1) shift the awareness away from the real risk in deployed technology and onto less risk-informative enterprise demands, (2) quickly split critical security resources into diverging functions (e.g., owing to the measure, collecting data for the measure, refining the math, communicating the measure up and down the organization) without considering the operational impact or the ability to mature and adapt simpler measures over time, and (3) develop a tendency to strive for perfection up front rather than a gradual and less-overwhelming maturity of risk-informative measures that are "good enough" for a first run and mature over time.

As with any long-term program, measures must evolve over time—beginning somewhere and aspiring to end somewhere more precise once the problem is better understood. To that end, good measures mature over time as the organization better understands its cybersecurity posture and aligns reliable data and practices to address the risk. Using basic measures to quantify uncertainty and appropriate risk mitigation activities is useful when applying a prestructured risk framework. Appropriate allocation of risk measures can initially inform decisions around appropriate risk coverage; then, tackling the resources needed to achieve the intended outcome becomes easier.

Apply Appropriate Resources

Identifying and applying the appropriate resources for any given risk area, activity, or initiative is an area where almost every organization struggles. Proper risk mitigation measures help in this area, as the feedback measures help inform where resources are most needed. For example, allocating resources can include critical performance areas (e.g., the performance of cybersecurity incident handlers or a change in service-level agreements), high-risk areas (e.g., respond/recover capabilities or employee behavior), and organizational communication areas (e.g., the number of response plans tested in one year). A mature program may be measured for value with a fundamental understanding of the risks associated with performance.

Drive for Value

Organizations are at widely different comfort levels with feedback measures. Some don't use them; others only operate by them. When organizations develop a strong comfort level with measures in security, the utility of measuring value begins to emerge around developing a point of view on how much to invest in mitigating risk. Insights begin to surface on key strategic topics, like the value or utility of your security investment or the value of certain controls.

Mature cybersecurity feedback measures can help inform a level of investment needed to understand exactly where the organizational risk line is (i.e., risk tolerance, relative to spending). This information can help define where the real line is for cybersecurity risk within the organization. Insights may be measured, for example, to address questions such as "How much would an adversary have to spend to get into our system?" or "How much do we have to invest to make it hard for an attacker to get into our system?"

The real benefits of these insights come from measuring and communicating less expensive but highly useful security measures that reduce risk in unintuitive ways. For example, deploying very basic controls that raise the bar for attackers (e.g., file access control, multifactor authentication, user access controls) requires very low investment. Measuring, managing, and communicating risk reduction around these examples can highlight the real value of high-impact items within a security program.

Two pitfalls should be avoided to extract the real benefit in security programs through measures: unclear measures and striving for perfection.

Be Clear on What to Measure

Identifying clear security measures is a widely debated topic in the security community, and for a good reason: not everyone is clear on how to inform whom and about what. Chapter 6 provides a current point of view on measures; however, two baseline concepts on measures should be addressed now.

First, the resource investment made in measures should be less than the return received from what is measured. That is, spend more time and money on using the information provided by measures than on trying to find the perfect measure. Choosing informative measures is critical to providing actionable feedback across the organization over time.

Second, measures that "mature over time" are helpful to almost every organization; this is to say measure what is measurable now (e.g., reliable and relevant data, risk understanding of executives) with a clear definition or focus on what to measure later when reliable data is available. A good example of this may be the "number of employees demonstrating poor security behavior." The initial measure may start with how many people fail phishing campaigns, providing a risk indication of where a successful phishing event may occur. Later, this measure may mature to include employees who fail more than one phishing campaign and also have a data loss prevention (DLP) trigger, providing more risk insights into the actual behavior of employees.

The challenge is that many organizations stall when implementing proper cybersecurity measures: some because the real risk is not understood, some because technology drives the measures, and others because the data to feed measures is simply not available. The first two challenges may be solved—or at least informed—through the practices outlined in Chapters 4 and 5. The last challenge may be solved by introducing measures that may mature over time.

Avoid Chasing "Perfect" (It's Not That Valuable)

Cybersecurity is one area where the expression "better is the enemy of good enough" does not universally apply. However, a key pitfall in security is chasing perfection in any one area. A perfectly secure system is an asymptote, and no one is quite there yet. As new designs and new tests for security progress toward a more perfect system, solutions get closer to the asymptote. Conversely, the more time we spend on making improvements and features, the more flaws we may introduce.

Sounds challenging? Chasing perfection is challenging, and pursuing it takes a lot of resources. In security risk management, the key question is: what amount of time and effort should we invest to achieve a reasonable level of security against an attack? This is the "good enough" (or risk-tolerant) line that makes the most sense for organizations.

Chasing perfection has its challenges and may not end up achieving the overall intent. In security, trying to perfect one thing runs the risk of missing the big picture, leaving security gaps in other areas. A holistic approach to security, with reasonable and measurable goals, helps secure the whole system—this is the problem to be solved. The main thing to consider with measures is the overall value of all of the measures, collectively. The problem measures should aim to solve is: does organizational security rise to a level slightly above what attackers will spend to achieve their objectives?

PART II

The Solution

Keep in Mind

To best address cybersecurity risks, keep three questions in mind:

- **Understand**: What are your cybersecurity risks?

- **Manage**: How are you managing your cybersecurity risks?

- **Measure**: How are you measuring your cybersecurity risk reduction?

CHAPTER 4

Understanding the Problem

Introduction

Tying risk to critical assets is the core component of any cybersecurity risk management program. Understanding what attackers find valuable and what imperfections exist in the organization will help communicate risk and drive what safeguards the business is willing to resource.

Knowing which problem you are solving is the most critical part in solving any problem, and cybersecurity risk is no different. Spending time exploring the main issues helps ensure a crisp and accurate problem statement. This typically means asking probing questions within the organization to identify what others see as the problem, gathering facts and opinions (and knowing the difference between the two), and then agreeing upon a problem statement to solve, which categorically encompasses all the facts you have gathered.

Why spend time discussing problem-solving first? Solving the right problem (the right set of risks) in cybersecurity early can make all the difference between a *moderate event* that may be handled by security staff internally and a *full-blown incident* that may become a breach—leading to breach notification and lost confidence by the public. Solving the wrong problems leaves the real risks underrepresented and, therefore, openly exposed.

© Ryan Leirvik 2023
R. Leirvik, *Understand, Manage, and Measure Cyber Risk*,
https://doi.org/10.1007/978-1-4842-9319-5_4

Solving for the right risks means defining the problem while keeping up with what the business needs to operate. That is, the risk problem must be well-defined. This is a common challenge in security. Many times, immediate problems that surface are not always tied to a well-understood business risk, and these problems can easily become time-consuming distractions for problem-solving security teams. While solving an immediate problem sometimes can seem like a worthwhile endeavor, it is not always clear how it relates to the business or how it relates to protecting critical assets. For example, audit teams typically define a cyber problem as a set of costly fines and resolution-based resources the organization bears if it falls out of compliance (a.k.a. compliance risk). Contract teams typically define a cybersecurity problem as the ability to shift risk to vendors or contractors (a.k.a. third parties). Technology teams define a cyber problem as open vulnerabilities, bad passwords, and lack of perfect asset management. That is, each team typically will view their portion of the cyber risk. Individually, each team is not wrong. Collectively, however, each team's problem-solving efforts and association to the broader organizational problem are not always clear: impact to the organization due to critical assets at risk.

This is the lesson for truly understanding the risk associated with cybersecurity in any organization. Knowing what problem is being solved, and being clear about it, helps each team or contributor see how their part of the problem-solving (risk reduction or risk mitigation) plays into the overall solution of protecting what matters to the organization in achieving its mission. Communicating the risk as a single problem that impacts the organization as a whole has the power of resource alignment, pulling everyone together to solve one common goal, like the loss of, or damage to, critical assets.

Sounds simple? It is. Sounds easy? It's not. Focusing an entire organization on a well-defined cybersecurity problem is simple. Managing the efforts to solve the problem is hard. But following some basic rules helps make management easier.

Rules to Follow

The problem to solve is the protection of critical assets. After all, on asset classes, data is the most targeted asset in information security and typically gains the most attention that drives impact to the organization.[1] Most organizations, however, struggle to identify what is critical. One approach is to follow five basic rules.

RULES TO FOLLOW: UNDERSTANDING THE PROBLEM

Five basic rules in understanding cybersecurity risk.

TAKEAWAYS

- **Rule 1**: Be clear on the problem (critical assets are at risk).
- **Rule 2**: Settle on a definition of *risk*.
- **Rule 3**: Settle on a definition of *critical*.
- **Rule 4**: Inventory and categorize the *critical* assets.
- **Rule 5**: Identify the risks to the critical assets.

Be Clear About the Problem (Critical Assets Are at Risk)

Establishing a crisp and clear problem statement can be wildly rewarding when solving complex cybersecurity problems. A clear statement can set the vision and goal for one unified approach to overall enterprise cybersecurity—providing the critical ability for understanding and articulating the current state of risk. Organizations that put forth a single clear definition of the problem have a greater chance for success in implementing effective cybersecurity programs—not as a *technical management* problem but as a *business risk management* problem.

A business risk problem may sound something like "protect critical assets that may harm the enterprise if compromised." A definition such as this provides an opportunity to define a supporting operational goal,

---

[1] Notwithstanding networks and applications as part of critical infrastructure.

something like "zero loss of critical data" or "zero compromise of critical assets." One crisp statement, such as these, can become a focal point for a clear problem to solve, or objective to meet, in any cyber risk program. This type of a sharp statement sets the vision, useful for management to apply supporting guidelines around understanding the assets requiring protection.

So what exactly is critical, and how might critical assets be defined? Just as with management frameworks, no one definitive statement fits all organizations. For example, some organizations define assets as simply data and systems. Others define asset classes more exclusively as data, devices, applications, networks, and users.[2] However, one approach universally helps define critical assets for almost all organizations: determining the organizational impact should the asset be accessed, manipulated, or used in an unauthorized manner. It's the *impact* to the organization that helps clearly determine what is truly critical. This means the organization first needs to settle on a definition of risk.

Settle on a Definition of *Risk*

Before diving into *critical* assets, a clear definition of cybersecurity risk is necessary. Since *enterprise risk* defines why the manipulation of a particular resource or event could be a liability to the organization, many organizations have a non-cybersecurity risk definition. Settling on a cybersecurity risk definition, therefore, requires a link to the enterprise/organizational risk management process—ensuring both definitions clearly articulate organizational risk for appropriate organizational functions of the enterprise[3], cybersecurity being just one. Settling on a risk

---

[2] Sounil Yu uses and advocates strongly for these crisp and mutually exclusive asset classes. More information may be found at https://cyberdefensematrix.com.

[3] See "Step 5f" later in this chapter on how to make the link to enterprise risk management.

definition has the added benefit of "demystifying" some of the common terms typically discussed when addressing cyber events.

For example, NISTIR 7621 Revision 1 (a.k.a. NISTIR 7621r1) "Small Business Information Security: The Fundamentals" offers a helpful way to define cybersecurity threats, vulnerabilities, and risks to the enterprise. "Risk is a function of threats, vulnerabilities, the likelihood of an event, and the potential impact such an event would have to the [organization]."[4] Figure 4-1 is an illustrative diagram of cybersecurity risk adopted from this definition.

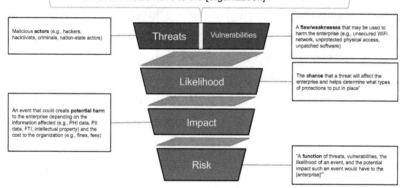

Figure 4-1. *Defining cybersecurity risk using NISTIR 7621r1*

Providing this type of organizationally recognized definition of risk offers a starting point for understanding what *risk* needs to be addressed. With a risk definition acknowledgment in place, a more formalized approach for categorizing what is *critical* may be pursued to manage the risk.

---

[4] This definition, quoted text, and corresponding diagram (displaying the relationship between threats, vulnerabilities, impact, and likelihood) is published in NISTIR 7621 Revision 1 "Small Business Information Security: The Fundamentals".

Settle on a Definition of *Critical*

Defining the term *critical* for the organization is an essential prerequisite for managing the risk; after all, it is a fundamental component to understanding exactly what needs to be properly managed. In most organizations, this is not an easy task. Individual business units, individual employees, and groups of executives typically have their own idea of which organizational asset is critical. These ideas are often largely based on their view of what they need to perform and not necessarily on what the organization relies on to operate.

In short, not every organizational asset is critical, and not all assets are technology-based. What is critical to one business unit, or single person, is not necessarily critical to the organization. Also, the organization may be heavily reliant on a resource that is not technological and may not intuitively be viewed as a cybersecurity risk.[5]

A common pitfall in defining critical assets for any organization is failing to distinguish between what individuals *think* is critical (to them or their job function) and what is *actually* critical to the operation of the organization, that is, the critical function or resource that the organization relies on to achieve its core objectives. The inability to clearly separate the two can put undue strain on organizational risk management, as the practical effort of clearly defining what is organizationally critical tussles with the social effort of accommodating individual desires.

Examples of this are individual work products or resources that individuals rely upon to simply perform well at their job (e.g., particular algorithms, certain analytical data). The inability to distinguish between what is critical to the organization and what is critical for individual performance paves a directionally inaccurate path toward protecting all

---

[5] Risk could impact "organizational operations (including mission, functions, image, or reputation), organizational assets, or individuals," according to NIST SP 800-37 Revision 2.

assets, rather than the protection of assets that attackers might consider targeting and that may create a crisis in the organization if maliciously manipulated. When organizations fall into this trap, the clear prioritization of programs and activities becomes overwhelming. This trap distracts from what is critical, pointing this important effort toward a major pitfall: trying to protect everything. Organizations that fall into this trap are at risk of manifesting the proclamation "to protect everything is to protect nothing."[6]

How to avoid this trap? One way is to "flip the problem" and take the perspective away from inside the organization and view it from outside the organization; view the problem from the attacker's perspective, not the organization's perspective.

Attackers have an objective or a goal and look for ways to achieve that objective.[7] One overused but effective tool is the Cyber Kill Chain model,[8] providing a high-level model to understand how adversaries plan attacks for a particular target, like an organization. An alternative view is the MITRE ATT&CK framework. Looking at critical assets through this lens may help focus resources based on a hypothesis of certain attacker skills. Figure 4-2 is an applied example of the Cyber Kill Chain in how an attacker plans an attack.

---

[6] Who originally said, "He who defends everything, defends nothing"? Frederick the Great? Napoleon? Sun Tzu (changed in translation to English)? None of this book's contributors were there at the time; however, the meaning is understood for sure: focusing on protecting everything distracts from focusing on the items that matter.

[7] At this point the divine manifestation of the threat as the key player in the risk should strike like a lightning bolt, forming in the mind a powerful line from threat to vulnerability to risk. You're welcome.

[8] Originally known as the "intrusion kill chain", the Cyber Kill Chain model is attributed to Lockheed-Martin Corporation and illustrates how computer attacks may occur in stages.

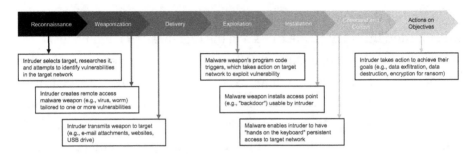

Figure 4-2. *An applied example of an attack plan using the Cyber Kill Chain model*

Taking the attacker's perspective is a useful way to help distinguish between what is useful inside the company and what might be useful outside the company. To help further this distinction for critical and non-critical assets, some organizations find it helpful to categorize these views into three different viewpoints:

- **Inside-out**: What do internal employees believe to be critical? Tally or categorize each asset and then ask this question: how do these assets contribute to the core mission? It should be apparent that not all assets are sensitive enough to significantly impact the business if affected. These are not critical.

- **Outside-in**: What might attackers/adversaries find valuable? Tally or categorize each asset valuable to an attacker, and then ask this question: what harm would come if an attacker successfully gained access to these assets? These are the critical asset classes.

- **Organizational**: Apply an organizational risk focus to what is truly critical. Of the assets in the critical asset classes, what company property will harm the organization in terms of reputation, revenue, or costs if lost or tampered with? These are the critical assets, and they need constant, successful defense—every time.

A crisp definition of *critical* means clearly identifying all assets that will significantly impact the core objectives should the assets escape, be tampered with, or be used in an unauthorized manner.[9] With this in mind, the focus turns away from "what is important" to a business unit or a person and toward "what is dire" to the organization, providing a formalized approach for addressing and categorizing actual critical assets.

For example, one may apply the three viewpoints to just one asset category. Figure 4-3 illustrates an inside-out and outside-in perspective for the *data* category.

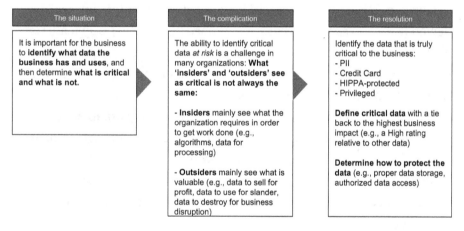

Figure 4-3. *Applying an insiders and outsiders view to data*

For many organizations, the process of defining what is critical can take some time. The "Inventory and Categorize Critical Assets" and the "Identify the Risks to These Critical Assets" sections in this chapter both

---

[9] Other assets notwithstanding, this is information security. Again, US Code Title 44 defines information security as "The protection of information and information systems from unauthorized access, use, disclosure, disruption, modification, or destruction in order to provide confidentiality, integrity, and availability."

feature steps that walk through the seemingly arduous process. In a pinch, or for smaller organizations, you can jump directly to Step 5c to identify what is most valuable to the organization.

Inventory and Categorize Critical Assets

Identifying critical assets (e.g., data, devices, applications, networks, users) is mandatory to understand an organization's cybersecurity risks. Knowing what harm a cybersecurity event could do to an organization requires anticipating the potential harm an event could inflict on certain organizational possessions. The impact depends on the possible data affected (e.g., PHI data, PII data, FTI, intellectual property), devices affected (e.g., web cams, displays, machinery, appliances), applications affected (e.g., key services, software), users affected (e.g., employees), as well as the overall resource drain on the organization (e.g., fines, fees, uninsured ransom, actual money loss).

Pinpointing these types of potential harm-inducing organizational assets offers managers the ability to understand them and then manage them and then measure the associated risk to the business operations should these assets be compromised in some way. This may sound obvious, conceptually, but routinely practicing it is not apparent in many organizations.

Many organizations struggle with just how to inventory and manage items of value within an organization. In large organizations, the sheer amount of information relative to any particular asset may be overwhelming. Also, simple recommendations on implementation management tools, like an asset management system or a configuration management database (CMDB), sound easy as a concept outside the organization. But inside the organizations, employees in charge of management activities routinely express just how difficult it is to discover and properly manage all the assets in the organization.[10] Layer in the ability to distinguish between what is vital from what is not. The request for supporting resources begins to climb as the challenges of identifying the authoritative asset owner and managing updates begin to take hold.

Buckling under the weight of asset management is a risk worthy of executive consideration before tackling the effort. Time is best spent considering the costs and implications, which, in turn, should settle on the value of the effort. One of the clear value propositions is the ability to manage and protect any critical asset.

Where to begin to execute the simplest, but arguably the most difficult, process of asset inventory? At a high level, the following basic steps may serve as a guideline in the asset definition journey.

How to Inventory and Categorize Critical Assets

Take the following steps to inventory and categorize critical assets:

- **Step 1**. Acknowledge that asset management is hard.

- **Step 2**. Develop the business case.

- **Step 3**. Define the asset classes (i.e., data, devices, applications, networks, users).

- **Step 4**. Collect and inventory assets into each asset class.

- **Step 5**. Identify the most critical.

---

[10] Based on years of experience, IT management employees have expressed just how hard it is to implement and maintain a truly real-time comprehensive IT asset management system. No empirical data was discovered to support this opinion; however, the claim seems to stand on its own merit.

Step 1. Acknowledge That Asset Management Is Hard

First, settle on the notion that asset management is not easy. The goal is to categorize, document, and maintain IT assets well enough to manage them in a central, repeatable fashion. The cost and implication of starting this process should be considered beforehand, in a business case, along with an identified team of individuals who will own the effort. Many organizations simply *do not* perform asset management well. Many organizations skip building a business case and move directly to a tool that promises to solve all asset problems. The challenge this presents is jumping into a solution before determining what the problem is.

Keep in Mind

One note before jumping in: A good number of factors contribute to the difficulty of properly managing assets: the aggregation of legacy documentation around maintaining the current inventory, the manual or semi-manual process of updating legacy documents, the lack of appropriate tools/tooling, and the simple lack of a current inventory altogether. One of the growing complexities is the proliferation of cloud services; typically, unaffiliated organizations (a.k.a. third parties) are used to help process or store data. Third parties are often overlooked or not readily identifiable in traditional on-premise asset management tooling. The tools are typically programmed to scan only permitted network locations or rely solely on agents to report findings.

The overwhelming majority of these factors may be overcome and managed by a thoughtful approach to defining asset classes, collecting inventory, and defining what is critical. This helps move away from the immediate reliance on tools[11] to figure out what is needed and to better understand the problem before applying the tool. To get there, asking the hard questions is needed to begin the process of defining your assets, ultimately helping with the identification, remediation, and containment in the event of a cyber incident or breach.

Organizational leaders who acknowledge that the asset management process is not easy have an easier time developing a business case to identify critical assets.

To get started, develop the business case before jumping into asset classes. This helps with the identification, remediation, and containment in the event of an incident.

Step 2. Develop the Business Case

Second, develop a business case that helps crisply communicate the problem being solved and the major considerations (e.g., costs, possible solutions, implications) to executives. Doing so demonstrates the thinking and the expected value of the effort. When complete, the implications of adopting, inventorying, and maintaining an asset management system should be clear.

To get started, clarify the dimensions needed for consideration in a business case. These include at a minimum, but are not limited to, the following:

- The problem statement

- A clear description of the current situation

- Example types of assets at risk within the organization

---

[11] This includes the problems many seek to solve with a tool or a suite of tools to display inventory management in a nice dashboard and work tickets.

- Potential harm or organizational impact (should types of assets be affected)

- Possible solutions to address the situation

- Resources needed for each solution

- Cost analysis of resources to reduce harm/impact (i.e., the value of a program)

- Final recommendation

Consider unique business case elements for each dimension that may help clarify business demands. This may include determining the teams that are already involved, the data that has been identified, which asset categories have gone unnoticed, and which resources are needed to assist in the journey.

ServiceNow, a CMDB provider, offers a thorough approach to IT asset management (ITAM) and software asset management (SAM). Their ebook, *The Gorilla Guide to Achieving IT Assessment Success*,[12] provides objectives for organizations to consider when establishing business cases.

Should the business case demonstrate the possible value of moving forward with a robust asset management plan, it is time to move on to the next step: defining asset classes.

Step 3. Define Your Asset Classes

Third, define the classes that will be used to categorize assets in the organization. The business case should have pointed out certain types of assets at risk within your organization. Using the classes from the business case as a start, develop a list of comprehensive categories that are mutually

---

[12] The Gorilla Guide to Achieving IT Asset Management Success is at www.servicenow.com/lpebk/gorilla-guide-it-asset-management.html.

exclusive of each other and collectively exhaustive of the whole ("mutually exclusive, collectively exhaustive").[13]

No one definitive set fits all organizations perfectly. For example, some organizations define assets as simply data and systems, while others define asset classes more exclusively as data, devices, applications, networks, and users. For this illustration, the latter will be used.

Begin with a definition of each class, and strongly focus on a crisp definition of each asset class—the shorter, the better. Developing a concise definition forces everyone involved to write information that is usually taken for granted: or largely "in the heads" of others, but not explicitly stated. The value of a crisp definition is crystal clear, differentiating asset classes from one another in distinctive ways. Figure 4-4 is a simple worksheet[14] to capture the fundamentals of the assets needed for an asset management process.

---

[13] Barbara Minto created an elegant and effective way to group ideas into separate pieces that are mutually exclusive of each other and collectively exhaustive of the whole. Check out "The Minto Pyramid Principle: Logic in Writing, Thinking and Problem Solving" (www.barbaraminto.com) to find out how you think and solve problems.

[14] Plenty of tools exist to help in this process. But using a simple worksheet first helps outline and raise the possible complexities of the effort, before moving towards a more robust management practice supported by a tool or a mature process.

ASSET CLASS	DEFINITION	ASSET	ASSET ID	LOCATION	OWNER
DEVICES	...				
APPLICATIONS	...				
NETWORKS	...				
DATA	...				
USERS	...				

Figure 4-4. *Simple worksheet to capture asset fundamentals*

Once complete with definitions, these categories may be redefined and expanded as they are tested during the discovery and accounting (inventory) process. As this process moves forward, it is important to remember that asset classes are not immovable. New categories may be created or existing ones redefined; developing a truly exclusive and collectively exhaustive asset class list is not entirely likely on the first attempt. The five classes used here may be useful as a starting point.

Step 4. Collect and Inventory in Each New Asset Class

Develop a satisfactory record, with responsible owners, for each asset discovered in the organization. The goal is to identify the type of asset, its whereabouts, and the owner so proper management may be applied to each and sufficient security may be applied to assets deemed critical.

With the asset classes identified, an inventory can begin to take place including locations and ownership by title. Plenty of commercial products exist to help with this exercise. With the business case developed and asset classes defined at some level, the choice becomes to choose a tool or continue with an internally developed process. Either way, the important step is to collect and properly account for each new asset. Figure 4-5 illustrates completing a simple worksheet.

ASSET CLASS	DEFINITION	ASSET	ASSET ID	LOCATION	OWNER
DEVICES	Exact meaning of "Devices"	•TBD •TBD •TBD	•D-1 •D-2 •D-3	•LOC •LOC •LOC	•TITLE •TITLE •TITLE
APPLICATIONS	Exact meaning of "Applications"	•TBD •TBD •TBD	•A-1 •A-2 •A-3	•LOC •LOC •LOC	•TITLE •TITLE •TITLE
NETWORKS	Exact meaning of "Networks"	•TBD •TBD •TBD	•N-1 •N-2 •N-3	•LOC •LOC •LOC	•TITLE •TITLE •TITLE
DATA	Exact meaning of "Data"	•TBD •TBD •TBD	•DA-1 •DA-2 •DA-3	•LOC •LOC •LOC	•TITLE •TITLE •TITLE
USERS	Exact meaning of "Users"	•TBD •TBD •TBD	•U-1 •U-2 •U-3	•LOC •LOC •LOC	•TITLE •TITLE •TITLE

Figure 4-5. *Illustrative completion of the simple worksheet*

With the assets properly identified and accounted for in a workable structure, the process of determining which is most critical may begin.

Step 5. Identify the Most Critical Assets

Finally, pull into focus which assets are most critical. The objective here is to clarify which assets may harm the organization if tampered with or unauthorized access occurs and record them in a risk register (subsequent sections cover threat modeling and risk identification). For example, imagine this process has identified a particular data type as critical to the organization. In order to adequately protect this data type, additional analysis must occur to identify which systems this data resides on, individuals or adjacent systems that have access to this data, and the level of access the systems/individuals have to this critical data. Often when data is observed as a critical asset, many overlook how it is used and processed during normal business workflows, affecting what might be done to mitigate the risks.

With this baseline understanding of "what is critical to the business's operations," clarity is now formed around what needs to be protected for the business's operations. Clarity here means that protection mechanisms may be focused once the risk to these assets is understood.

Identify the type of criticality needed within the organization. Options range from highly restricted, confidential, internal use only, and public to risk exposure levels high, medium, and low and to simply critical and non-critical. Each organization should settle on the appropriate criticality definition, largely based on industry standards, regulations, or peer-group use.

Figure 4-6 illustrates a risk register, a simple worksheet to capture asset fundamentals.

PRIORITY	ASSET ID	RISK	IMPACT	EXPOSURE	STATUS
1	D-1	•TBD	•TBD	H / M / L	•TBD
2	D-1	•TBD	•TBD	H / M / L	•TBD
3	D-3	•TBD	•TBD	H / M / L	•TBD
4	D-4	•TBD	•TBD	H / M / L	•TBD
5	D-5	•TBD	•TBD	H / M / L	•TBD

Figure 4-6. *Risk register for critical assets*

With the organizational assets categorized into critical and non-critical, the work of clearly anticipating the risks to these organizational elements may begin.

Identify the Risks to These Critical Assets

One of the key security elements is to anticipate what may cause harm to the assets that have been identified as critical; one needs to know what they are protecting from whom, naturally. Appropriately recognizing the risks is one way to sharpen the focus on what exactly to guard against. The challenge is that a critical asset list without assigned risks can become a daunting task. One way to tackle this is to follow five steps after completing the critical asset definition steps. These next five steps help home in on the real risks faced by these critical assets.

How to Identify the Risks to These Critical Assets

To begin identifying the risks to the critical assets, take these steps (continued from inventory):

- **Step 5a**. Perform a threat analysis.

- **Step 5b**. Discover vulnerabilities.

- **Step 5c**. Anticipate the business impact of an event.

- **Step 5d**. Pull it together in the risk register and keep it updated.

- **Step 5e**. Know the Applicable Laws and Regulations.

- **Step 5f**. Connect cybersecurity risk to enterprise risk.

Step 5a. Perform a Threat Analysis

Recall that "risk is a function of threats, vulnerabilities, the likelihood of an event, and the potential impact such an event would have to the [organization]."[15] Since the main objective is to identify and reduce the risk, the threat requires some analysis in this step; this is the proverbial outside-in view, or the attackers' view, of the organization.

Since a developed point of view on assets within the organization has been established, performing a threat model is the next step in discovering what potential threats exist to the assets, setting the stage for a look into the vulnerabilities that the threat will abuse to their advantage.

But first, what is a threat model? A threat model identifies what is critically important, prioritizes which attacks would be most damaging, and forces a comprehensive analysis of items within scope. Why perform a threat analysis using a threat model? Simply put: verification and validation. Building a proper threat model provides a documented set of all *security-relevant systems* that have been verified. This includes unhandled security issues for proper remediation and severity ratings for prioritization. Overall, the model provides visibility into current and future security issues based on the possible threats against the system under analysis.

A proper threat analysis using a threat model takes some effort. Like first-time asset managers, many first-time threat modelers ask whether having a threat model is worth all the time it takes to build one. If the essence of security risk is anticipating the threats that might take advantage of organizational vulnerabilities, identifying the threats is crucial in knowing what prevention methods may be followed. Building and maintaining a threat model can provide threat and threat-related information to inform proper mitigation methods.

---

[15] This definition is published in NISTIR 7621 Revision 1. The word business is replaced here with organization to widen the scope to any organization.

To get started, identify the threat model that works best for the organization and asset classes. Many threat models exist, and the one that best fits the organization fits the types of systems, or assets, under test—that is, the data, devices, applications, networks, and users affected by the threats.

One threat model example is Trike,[16] which is open source and offers a threat modeling methodology with two implementation tools (i.e., spreadsheet and desktop). A model for potential threats is STRIDE, which is a mnemonic for remembering the following threat categories:

- **S**poofing

- **T**ampering

- **R**epudiation

- **I**nformation disclosure

- **D**enial of service

- **E**levation of privilege

While Trike is a helpful methodology, its implementation and resources may challenge those new to it. In this case, STRIDE may be a helpful "model of threats" resource if the scope is focused specifically on software security.

---

[16] Naturally, since this is a risk book, the first recommendation is a threat model that offers "a unified conceptual framework for security auditing from a risk management perspective through the generation of threat models in a reliable, repeatable manner," according to Paul Saitta, Brenda Larcom, and Michael Eddington. More information is at www.octotrike.org.

Other threat modeling options exist for exploration into the best organizational fit to help think like an attacker. This includes OCTAVE,[17] PASTA,[18] and many others.

With a proper method of modeling threats, the next steps are to walk through the threat model using the chosen model process.

How to Walk Through an Overview of a Threat Model

It is helpful to understand the components of a threat model before developing one:[19]

- First, start with identifying anyone who may interact with any portion of the system and determine if they should be considered a potential attacker.

- Next, enumerate the system components along with who should have access to each component.

- Then, rank each possible unauthorized access or denial of authorized access in terms of the threat that it poses to the system.

---

[17] A "risk-based strategic assessment and planning technique for security" offered by Christopher Alberts in 2003 in the paper "Introduction to the OCTAVE Approach" at Carnegie Mellon University, Pittsburg, PA.

[18] More information may be found in *Risk Centric Threat Modeling: Process for Attack Simulation and Threat Analysis* by Tony UcedaVelez and Marco M. Morana (Wiley, 2015).

[19] According to Adam Nichols, security researcher extraordinaire. Laying out the components before getting started sets the understanding for creating clear security objectives based on impact to the organization; which, arguably, is the main point of this book.

- From here, create formal security objectives to ensure the focus of all remaining efforts remains on the most important threats and does not get distracted by minor security issues. This is vital, as it is important that the resources allocated to security review are spent based on impact to the organization.

Step 5b. Discover Vulnerabilities

A vulnerability, or a way in, is what the threats, or threat actors, exploit to act on their objectives. When understanding what threats might be targeting the organization, vulnerability discovery is an essential next step.

Before jumping in, recall that all technology is flawed and that every flaw may be a significant source for vulnerabilities in the organization by a malicious actor. Typically, the reaction to this thinking is around how data could be vulnerable (e.g., stolen, corrupted, poisoned, manipulated) either in storage or in transit or processing. Data is one of the most discussed targets for attackers. However, data is not the only target; keep in mind the asset categories. Each asset category with an organization has an element of risk, as previously defined in the organizational critical asset worksheet. Each asset should have a method to discover, triage, and remediate known and unknown vulnerabilities. It is essential to view all assets, just as it is essential not to blur the lines between vulnerability discovery, prioritization of known vulnerabilities, and remediation. Not all vulnerabilities are known at any given time. Not all vulnerabilities have an investigated impact (e.g., proof of concept, depth of criticality within the infrastructure). Not all vulnerabilities have remediation (e.g., a patch). Without a proper mechanism for managing all assets in the organization, not all assets are reachable for either vulnerability discovery, prioritization, or remediation. In short, vulnerability discovery and remediation are the centerpieces to security; without an open vulnerability, the attackers have a more challenging way in. So the focus here is on the first step: discovery.

A vulnerability discovery process for each critical asset, or at least asset class, is crucial. No one organization is the same, and each organization has a unique set of critical assets that require vulnerability discovery. For example, two industries with differing vulnerability discovery approaches are energy (private) and public services (civil). Both are industries in which the loss of control of an asset would be highly damaging to the system owner, including power generation and emergency medical services.

But discovering vulnerabilities in IT network resources may have a different prioritization. A low-level denial-of-service (DoS) attack targeting external IT communications is somewhat less critical for a power generator[20] than the same type of DoS attack on an emergency medical system, which may cripple the life-saving service. The focus on discovery is asset-dependent.

First, know the assets in the organization. This data should be available in the asset management process of the organization.[21]

Second, amass information about these assets from relevant resources inside and outside of the organization. Many resources exist for outside information on specific assets (e.g., national vulnerability database) and inside the organization (e.g., static and dynamic scanners). Arguably, the most important step is collecting the relevant information about the assets in the environment to set the stage for selecting the proper data and information to analyze.

---

[20] OK, somewhat annoying. Details do matter. For illustrative purposes, this scenario assumes (1) a low-level DoS attack on the IT external network and (2) legitimate denied access to IT does not affect the OT side during generation. However, the attack acting as a distraction for something else is another topic.

[21] Including Software Bill of Materials. (See "Step 5d. Link a Software Bill of Materials to the TPRM Program" in Chapter 5.).

Third, perform an analysis of the asset-relevant vulnerability information. How important is the vulnerability? A common method for determining previously unidentified criticality is the Common Vulnerability Scoring System (CVSS).[22] It is a published standard for capturing vulnerability characteristics and assigning a numerical severity score. Another method is to use a scoring system bespoke to the organization that considers the affected organizational assets and overall impact on operations. Either way, assigning a relative, relatable, known value to the asset-specific vulnerability that indicates possible impact is imperative when managing and ultimately remediating the vulnerability. For example, publicly disclosed vulnerabilities may be assigned a Common Vulnerabilities and Exposures (CVE) identifier to help share vulnerability information if submitted for a CVE; however, not all vulnerabilities are publicly disclosed or submitted.

At this point, vulnerability discovery ends, and vulnerability management begins.[23] Organizations with strong vulnerability management practices will integrate all aspects of the vulnerability management process, from discovery to remediation. In this case, the next two steps are to prioritize a set of remediation actions for the vulnerabilities based on severity and then ensure someone owns the remediation efforts.

Overall, the main objective is to discover, triage, and remediate. But it all starts with discovery.

---

[22] The custodian of the CVSS is the Forum of Incident Response and Security Teams (FIRST). Detailed information on the latest version and changes may be found at www.first.org/cvss.

[23] For most organizations, vulnerability management is one practice that encompasses discovery, triage, and mitigation. Vulnerability discovery is simply the beginning of a wider management practice.

Step 5c. Anticipate the Business Impact of an Event

Understanding the impact of a cybersecurity event means knowing what happens to the organization when the confidentiality, integrity, or availability security objectives for specific assets are affected. This is where a business impact analysis is helpful.

One way to quickly address this is to use simple-to-calculate, spend-to-cost-avoidance measures to prove ROI, like in NISTIR 7621r1:

- Lost access/lost work

- Fines/penalties

- Legal activities

- Incident recovery

- Lost business/reputation loss (trust)

First, choose the proper impact categories that best fit the organization and a repository for the data. Figure 4-7 is a worksheet illustration containing all five of the impact categories, as borrowed from the NISTIR 7621r1 section on determining the value of your information.[24] These selected impact categories may be helpful as a starting point for almost any organization and may change or adapt over time, as needed.

---

[24] Impact categories should be customized to best fit the organization and/or the industry. The impact categories used here are largely borrowed from NISTIR 7621 Revision 1 section on determining the "value of your information"; they may be used as a starting point for almost any organization.

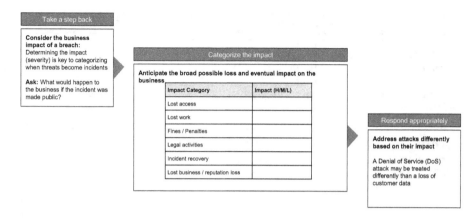

Figure 4-7. *Illustration of impact categories*

Second, complete a worksheet focusing on one asset class at a time: for example, the data asset class.

In the data asset class, an event that could potentially harm the enterprise depends on the data affected[25] (e.g., PHI data, PII data, FTI, intellectual property) and the cost to the organization (e.g., fines, fees). This NISTIR points out a bit more qualitative way to categorize these data sets. Figure 4-8 shows a method of assigning a dollar amount for each category or a scale of 0–3 or none, low, moderate, and high when dollar amounts are unavailable.

---

[25] Affected, for this example, means stolen/lost/made public, manipulated in any form, or rendered unavailable.

Data Asset	Impact Category

(1) Chose each data type for impact assessment:
- PII
- HIPAA-protected
- Credit card
- Privileged

(2) Categorize each data type using:
- 0 for "none"
- 1 for "low"
- 2 for "moderate"
- 3 for "high"

(3) Prioritize for protection by impact score
- Highest Score = highest priority

(4) Repeat for other asset classes by impact score

Asset Type: Data

Impact Category	Impact (H/M/L)
	Data Type:_____
Lost access	
Lost work	
Fines / Penalties	
Legal activities	
Incident recovery	
Lost business / reputation loss	

Data Type _____ Impact Score:	

Impact-based Priority	

Figure 4-8. *Illustration of the dollar amount for each category*

Many times, however, conversions from qualitative approaches to quantitative measures are often not easily performed, for example, where actual or relative dollar amounts are unavailable or regulated data is not affected. In these cases, using the simplified impact categories provides a sufficient starting point.

Large organizations face a major challenge with multiple business units identifying and aggregating risks from the technical to the executive levels. Some organizations address this by federating this simple approach across business units to roll up into one aggregate. The benefit of a standardized scoring system becomes critical for prioritization.

This simple approach helps identify the impact of a cybersecurity event and helps answer the inevitable questions around how much a breach costs. The results of this approach may be used to inform the impact category of the risk register.

Now that asset classes are defined with owners, the potential risk to each asset is acknowledged, organizational impact levels are anticipated, and all the information may be pulled together into a risk register to manage and track the cybersecurity risks.

Fully understanding the risk is great. Documenting the risk for tracking and mitigation against core business objectives is even better. Building and maintaining a risk register to organize and manage risk through action awareness is even better than that.

Step 5d. Pull It Together in the Risk Register and Keep It Updated

First, choose a format for the risk register that works within the organization. A bit of systems thinking is useful here, as update and maintenance considerations should include how data will enter and exit the register and where authoritative data owners reside within the organization, as well as verify register updates, monitor access, and include which computing systems authorized user access.

A decent number of options exist to start on a risk register. Plenty of commercial products exist to fit what works best in the organization. Figure 4-9 is a simplified illustration of a risk register.

PRIORITY	ASSET ID	RISK	IMPACT	EXPOSURE	STATUS
1	D-1	•TBD	•TBD	H / M / L	•TBD
2	D-1	•TBD	•TBD	H / M / L	•TBD
3	D-3	•TBD	•TBD	H / M / L	•TBD
4	D-4	•TBD	•TBD	H / M / L	•TBD
5	D-5	•TBD	•TBD	H / M / L	•TBD

Figure 4-9. *Illustration of a risk register*

Second, determine an organizational owner for the entire risk register. This is the position (not the person) that ensures the pragmatic management, communication, and mitigation tracking of the risk. A database of risk is only as good as its effectiveness. Assigning a clear ownership structure to the information required to fully approach the risk helps ensure that the risk register effort remains relevant.

Step 5e. Know the Applicable Laws and Regulations

By now, *critical assets* should be a well-understood term. Conditions that may put these critical assets at risk should also be well understood, making it clear that cybersecurity contains components of information security (i.e., protecting critical assets) and computer security (i.e., protecting mostly all computer systems, online and offline). Understanding this helps recognize and acknowledge the laws and regulations that apply to assets under the organization's care.

In all asset classes, intellectual property, personal/personnel data, computer systems, and other company assets are not only protected by certain laws, but their due care is as well. Many of these types of assets are targeted for criminal activity, national security, and even harassment. As custodians of these asset classes, organizations must provide sufficient protection, and many laws and regulations make that clear.

First, be clear on which laws and regulations apply within which operating locations. To best protect and defend protected assets and reduce the risk of penalties or fines, organizations need to consult legal and regulatory resources to best clarify applicable laws and regulations.

For example, breach notification laws clarify the obligation to notify persons affected by breaches involving their sensitive personal information. Also, required programs clarify the obligation to implement information security programs to protect the confidentiality, integrity, and accessibility security objectives for data (known as the *CIA triad*).

Legal counsel should be able to identify the applicable legislation for understanding compliance and associated fines. These may include the following:

- GDPR (requires covered entities to report breach notification within 72 hours of first having become aware of the breach—entities breaching the GDPR may be fined up to 4% of annual global revenue or €20 million, whichever is greater)

- Privacy Act of 1974

- California Consumer Privacy Act

- California Privacy Rights Act

- Gramm-Leach-Bliley Act, the Federal Trade Commission Act

- Fair Credit Reporting Act

- Payment Card Industry Data Security Standard (PCI DSS)

- SEC (enforces actions from violations affecting shareholders and investors)

Second, keep in mind that adversaries of national governments are state-sanctioned, and regulations for some organizations may not apply. The laws and regulations continue to take shape, as with any regulated domain. Diligence on new regulations[26] should be a quarterly agenda topic for legal counsel.

---

[26] Discussions and debates endure impacting national security for a nation state and commercial activity (see www.lawfareblog.com/ responsible-cyber-offense).

Step 5f. Connect Cybersecurity Risk to Enterprise Risk

With a clear definition of *cybersecurity risk*, connecting cybersecurity risk to the overall enterprise risk management (ERM) process is crucial for the organization to maintain an overall, or *enterprise*, view of related risks. Risk definitions within the organization should clearly articulate the risk relative to the specific functions of the enterprise, cybersecurity risk being just one. This is the ideal state. Many organizations struggle with setting definitions of risk as it relates to each function, leaving business functions to set independent definitions without a clear roll-up into an overall enterprise risk management function—this makes it tricky when understanding, managing, and measuring risk in different capacities of the organization. The important criteria for cybersecurity risk is that it nests within the definitions of—or is at least in alignment with—the organization's enterprise risk. A few simple steps may help get there.

First, identify what the organization defines as *risk*. Is the definition specific? Does the definition consider each part of the organization (i.e., organizational functions), or can it be applied to each part of the organization? If yes, then a clear linkage to the cybersecurity definition may be relatively trivial by linking the two definitions in the appropriate organizational policy and subsequent procedures. If not, then it may be worthwhile to raise the issue with the appropriate risk managers within the organization; it's likely worthwhile to settle on an "acceptable risk definition" for your organization so that the linkage may be made to cybersecurity risk and enterprise risk management.

If addressing enterprise risk becomes a topic of interest, or even redefining the organization's general risk definition, consideration must be made of each part of the organization—starting with the most important (plus the close first, second, third, etc.) risk in each of the organizational functions. For example, what is your accounting department thinking when they think about risk? (Literally, what is your accounting team thinking about when they think about risk?) Expect answers to risk questions to come back being department-focused, such as human resources suggesting "people" are the organization's biggest risk and finance suggesting "monetary value loss" as the biggest risk to the organization. Both are true... but one focuses on impact and the other something else. Just as a cybersecurity program is a function of the business—like human resources and finance—the definitions of risk need to represent the function as well as the whole, so that it may be accurately measured and mitigated. The overall objective is to have a common definition and understanding of risk at each functional level. One way to help gain traction on an overall definition is to focus on impact to the organization's overall mission.

Second, map the cybersecurity risk definition to the enterprise risk definition that fits the organization at each functional level. Then, layer in the cybersecurity program.

One helpful way to specifically link the cybersecurity program, as a functional area, to the enterprise[27] is to use the chosen cybersecurity guiding framework.[28] Commonly known frameworks serve as a guiding post to assist organizations in understanding their current maturity, filling in gaps where they may not have controls, and providing a road map to how to improve in the future (i.e., how to build your defenses to help mitigate, understand, or accept the risks for your enterprise). Continuing with the CSF use, a "crosswalk mapping" may be useful to understand how multiple frameworks might map together (e.g., NIST CSF, NIST 800-53, NIST 800-171, ISO 27001).

For example, if an organization follows the CSF as the guiding cybersecurity risk framework and also uses (or pursues) ISO 27001

---

[27] Recall, this is a book on cybersecurity risk, not enterprise risk management. Here, cyber risk rolling into your enterprise risk is the main objective.

[28] See Chapter 5 "Focus on One Framework".

(certification), such a mapping to security controls would help in the cybersecurity-to-enterprise risk relationship. These types of crosswalk mappings are quite the challenge—both labor and expertise intensive–but can pay significant dividends for the work invested. Using the base CSF as a starting point to inform the overall security program and then crosswalk mapping to ISO 27001, a linkage is created to view security controls coverage in the overall program by building off the work already in place and combining strong parts of two divergent approaches (i.e., one guide and one standard).

An example crosswalk mapping is demonstrated in Figure 4-10, serving as an example of how to compare both frameworks in a visual format, supporting the ISO 27001 certification process as well as understanding what controls are already in place with the CSF.

NIST CSF CATEGORY	NIST CSF SUB-CATEGORY	ISO 27001
Risk Management Strategy (ID.RM): The organization's priorities, constraints, risk tolerances, and assumptions are established and used to support operational risk decisions.	ID.RM-1: Risk management processes are established, managed, and agreed to by organizational stakeholders	4.3: Determining the scope of the information security management system
		4.4: Information security management system
		6.1.1: General
		6.1.2: Information security risk assessment
		6.2: Information security objectives and planning
		7.5.1: General
		7.5.3: Control of documented information
		9.3: Management review
		10.2: Continual improvement
		4.3: Determining the scope of the information security management system
		6.1.2: Information security risk assessment
		6.2: Information security objectives and planning
		7.4: Communication
		7.5.1: General
		7.5.2: Creating and updating
		7.5.3: Control of documented information
	ID.RM-2: Organizational risk tolerance is determined and clearly expressed	4.3: Determining the scope of the information security management system
		4.4: Information security management system
		6.1.1: General
		6.1.2: Information security risk assessment
		6.2: Information security objectives and planning
		7.5.1: General
		7.5.3: Control of documented information
		9.3: Management review
		10.2: Continual improvement

Figure 4-10. *NIST CSF to ISO 27001 crosswalk*

Understanding the Problem: A Recap

Overall, the inherent flaw in technology has created a security problem requiring work at both the engineering and management levels. But addressing information security is not a technical problem. It is an organizational risk problem. Vulnerabilities are used against assets to undermine the specific functions the asset is meant to support. This is a difficult concept for some to grasp. Complicating the issue is the communication challenge between technical problems and management, as clear, crisp definitions are needed for contested topics like *risk, critical,* and *critical assets.* Complicating the issue more is that technology solutions are not easy to follow for those without technical backgrounds; technology's complexity and pervasiveness continue to expand.

The real problem of understanding the risk works the same as any other problem: be clear on which problem is being solved (e.g., "organizational assets at risk of manipulation, theft, and compromise"). A clear, crisp problem statement can help organizations understand what problem they are solving in cybersecurity. If the key is to understand the problem well enough to find the risks and ultimately restore overall confidence in using information technology to support the organizational mission, then a clear understanding of the risk helps everyone manage it.

Recent Examples

There are many examples of organizations needing to develop a crisp and accurate definition of critical assets. This chapter provides four examples. The first example is an organization that aspired to set up and achieve the fundamental components of an initial program to get started. This example is carried through each of the sections, from understanding to measuring. Additional examples highlight successes and challenges.

Example 1. Getting Started with a Program

A medium-sized SaaS company servicing the growing mobility market hired a chief information security officer (CISO) to bring together a disparate security practice and set a foundation for a mature cybersecurity program. The board of directors asked the CEO to have a program in place before the end of the quarter. Without a formal process, the new CISO had a strong team but not much of an organized program.

Immediately the CISO set two goals: (1) establish a structured program around risk to the organization in just under three months, and (2) bring an actionable cyber risk–based decision discussion to the board in three months. Then, they went to work to define and stand up a program before the end of the quarter.

To help track progress toward the two goals, the CISO established a checklist like the one shown in Figure 4-11.

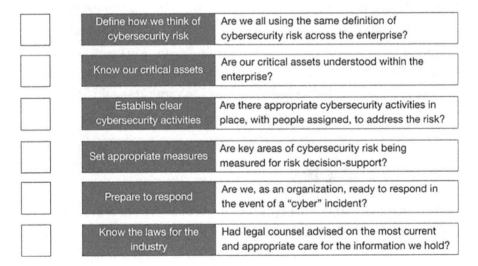

Figure 4-11. *Checklist for achieving goals toward a cybersecurity program establishment*

They first set out to settle on a definition of risk within the organization. Absent a common definition, the CISO gathered a team and started with the NISTIR 7621r1 definition. After some debate, the team of four dropped the use of likelihood. Given their size, they decided to address any threat that might take advantage of an existing vulnerability as likely and perhaps revisit the likelihood if the level of threats became too burdensome to properly address. Their definition of risk became "a function of the threats, the vulnerabilities, and the potential impact the two would have to our organization,"[29] as illustrated in Figure 4-12.

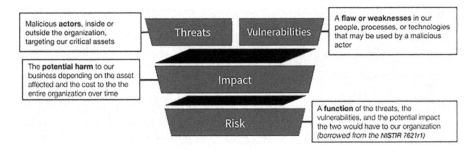

Figure 4-12. *The risk definition does not consider the likelihood of an event*

With the definition of risk, the team quickly crafted a risk management statement for the organization. They settled on a clear statement of zero impact on critical assets. Next, the definition of *critical* was required.

To settle on a definition of *critical*, the team again borrowed from the NISTIR 7621r1 impact categories. Figure 4-13 represents the model used to quickly identify critical definitions.

---

[29] Borrowed from NISTIR 7621 Revision 1.

Assets		Impact Category		
The process:		**Create one for each asset type:**		

(1) Chose each asset type for impact assessment:
- Data
- Devices
- Applications
- Networks
- Users

(2) Categorize each data type using:
- 0 for "none"
- 1 for "low"
- 2 for "moderate"
- 3 for "high"

(3) Prioritize for protection by impact score
- Highest Score = highest priority

Impact Category	Impact (H/M/L)
	Data Type: _____
Lost access	
Lost work	
Fines / Penalties	
Legal activities	
Incident recovery	
Lost business / reputation loss	

Data Type ____ Impact Score	
Impact-based Priority	

Figure 4-13. *Starter model for impact categories by asset class*

Since the model requires assets to be identified first, the team moved back to inventory assets; it became clear that asset management was unavoidable. After a month of rigorously investigating the documentation, interviews with potential asset owners, and physical inspections around offices and facilities (rogue devices, anyone?), the team developed an inventory worksheet that captured the current understanding of assets owned and managed by the organization. Figure 4-14 represents the first take at an asset inventory developing classes of data, devices, applications, networks, and users.

ASSET CLASS	DEFINITION	ASSET	ASSET ID	LOCATION	OWNER
DEVICES	Mechanical or electronic equipment	•Tivoli •Tolv-Ol •Havfrue	•D-001 •D-002 •D-003	•ML-1 •ML-1 •COP-1	•Dir. Tivoli •Dir. Ol •Sr. Mgr Hav
APPLICATIONS	Software performing a specific task	•W-Brod •Har •Ganre	•A-001 •A-002 •A-003	•ML-1 •ML-2 •ML-2	•Dir. Brod •Dir. Kunde •Dir. Kunde
NETWORKS	Connected computing resources	•Stroget •Sti-Vig •Vej-Vig	•N-001 •N-002 •N-003	•COP-1 •ML-1 •ML-2	•Sr. Mgr Nok •Sr. Mgr Nok •Sr. Mgr Nok
DATA	Quantities, characters, or symbols on which operations are performed	•PII •Credit Card •Privileged *(internal classification)*	•DA-1a •DA-2b •DA-3c	•Har •Har and W-Brod •Garne	•Dir. Kunde •Dir. Brod and Dir. Kunde •Dir. Kunde
USERS	People who work on, create, administer, and manage information systems	•Kober •Admin Cop •Admin ML •Vedlige	•U-1 •U-2 •U-3 •U-4	•Stroget •COP-1 •ML-1 •ML-2	•Sr. Mgr Nok •Dir. Nok •Dir. Nok •Dir. Nok

Figure 4-14. *Asset inventory by asset class (*asset, location, and owner are obfuscated)*

With the assets now defined and in inventory, the team returned their attention to the impact categories. This began the effort of determining the impact to the business should the confidentiality, availability, or integrity security objectives for assets be affected by an information security event. But first, they needed to prioritize what would most impact the organization. As a SaaS company servicing one industry, damage to information or information systems, regulatory fines and penalties, loss of information critical to running the business, and losing trust from clients were top considerations. After strong debate and analysis on topics, perfection lost out to "good enough" as the team progressed through all five asset classes of data, networks, users, applications, and devices. After the analysis, the team determined three areas—data, applications, and networks—as their top asset classes since they largely relied on data from customers for clients. Figure 4-15 represents the NISTIR 7621r1 model used to determine critical assets by asset category, this one for data.

Data Asset	Impact
(1) Chose each data type for impact assessment: - PII - HIPAA-protected - Credit card - Privileged **(2) Categorize each data type using:** - 0 for "none" - 1 for "low" - 2 for "moderate" - 3 for "high" **(3) Prioritize for protection by impact score** - Highest Score = highest priority **(4) Repeat for other asset classes by impact score**	**DATA TYPE: PII**

Impact Category	Impact (H/M/L)
	Data Type:_____
Lost access	
Lost work	
Fines / Penalties	
Legal activities	
Incident recovery	
Lost business / reputation loss	

Data Type _____ Impact Score:	

Impact-based Priority	

Figure 4-15. *Impact priority for one data type (i.e., PII)*

With the assets inventoried for better asset management and defined by value to the organization, the next was to set it up in a risk register. (Small companies and startups have the advantage of relative ease in identifying and categorizing assets.)

Figure 4-16 represents a portion of the risk register.

PRIORITY	ASSET ID	RISK	IMPACT	EXPOSURE	STATUS
1	DA-1a	• Confidentiality	• Regulatory fines and penalties • legal fees • Adverse reputation or loss of trust from customers	HIGH	• Establishing access controls (PAM Mgr activity)
2	DA-2b	• Confidentiality • Availability • Integrity	• Regulatory fines and penalties • Decreased productivity • Loss of information critical in running operations • Adverse reputation or loss of trust from customers	HIGH	• Establishing access controls (PAM Mgr activity)
3	DA-3c	• Confidentiality • Availability	• Decreased productivity • Loss of information critical in running operations • Legal fees (breach of contract) • Adverse reputation or loss of trust from customers	HIGH	• Establishing access controls (PAM Mgr activity) • Establishing Third-party controls (Legal activity)
...	...	...	...	...	...

Figure 4-16. *Top of a risk register, with data assets only*

This entire effort yielded the fundamentals for a cybersecurity program. The new CISO checked the top two items off the list and prepared the team to establish activities and measures. Figure 4-17 illustrates the checklist progress.

Figure 4-17. *Checklist marking the risk understanding portions completed*

Example 2. From Legacy "Perfection" to "Good Enough"

Asset management is paramount to driving an information security program's success. While the CISO described was able to get out ahead of the problem, some organizations are more reactive than proactive.

A large healthcare service provider was a victim of an attack. The lessons learned from the incident proved wholeheartedly the need for the organization to begin rethinking its approach to asset management. The board of directors of this large healthcare service provider made it the number one priority for the information security team to have this huge endeavor completed by the end of the year.

The organization went through several iterations trying to solve exactly how they would achieve this mammoth task. Unfortunately, they went straight for the tooling and struggled to get the tool to work the way it was intended to. After six months of struggling, the information security team and their CISO decided to hire outside consultants to help strategize and support their efforts.

After working with the consultants, the strategy became a bottom-up approach compared with the company's top-down plan (start with the tool). The organization still wanted their disparate manual legacy tracking moved to a CMDB by the end of the year. This left the teams to divide and conquer the asset classes (i.e., devices, applications, networks, data, and users).

Each team went off to collect assets from their assigned asset class. By dividing and conquering, the consultants and the organization's team members defined most of the assets within the asset classes and gave the asset a corresponding ID. The teams went about discovering assets in a variety of ways.

They started with existing data (i.e., spreadsheets and databases) to understand where each asset was currently sitting. Then they would validate if the asset was still in use or had been decommissioned (this goes for users too, but rather than decommissioned, the user's access was deprovisioned when the employee left the organization).

Next, the team conducted widespread interviews with individuals who had existing knowledge of the assets. The team would confirm the life cycle stage of the asset and update their inventory accordingly. Filling in an asset inventory from scratch can be daunting. Figure 4-18 shows how you can begin to form an accurate inventory for each of your asset classes.

ASSET CLASS	DEFINITION	ASSET	ASSET ID	LOCATION	OWNER
DEVICES	Exact meaning of "Devices"	• TBD • TBD • TBD	• D-1 • D-2 • D-3		
APPLICATIONS	Exact meaning of "Applications"	• TBD • TBD • TBD	• A-1 • A-2 • A-3		
NETWORKS	Exact meaning of "Networks"	• TBD • TBD • TBD	• N-1 • N-2 • N-3		
DATA	Exact meaning of "Data"	• TBD • TBD • TBD	• DA-1 • DA-2 • DA-3		
USERS	Exact meaning of "Users"	• TBD • TBD • TBD	• U-1 • U-2 • U-3		

Figure 4-18. *Asset inventory table (assets and asset IDs)*

After the teams felt they had a good understanding of the assets in each class, they went back and assigned the location and owners of *each* asset.

This step allows for a couple of things to happen: (1) collaboration with stakeholders to assign ownership (buy-in with the business) and (2) a second scan through the asset inventory to validate accuracy and completeness.

The second phase took less time because the teams already knew the individuals who claimed ownership of certain assets, making it easier to assign similar assets to certain teams. Filling in the inventory looks something like what is shown in Figure 4-19.

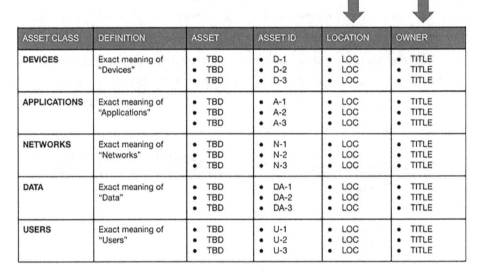

ASSET CLASS	DEFINITION	ASSET	ASSET ID	LOCATION	OWNER
DEVICES	Exact meaning of "Devices"	• TBD • TBD • TBD	• D-1 • D-2 • D-3	• LOC • LOC • LOC	• TITLE • TITLE • TITLE
APPLICATIONS	Exact meaning of "Applications"	• TBD • TBD • TBD	• A-1 • A-2 • A-3	• LOC • LOC • LOC	• TITLE • TITLE • TITLE
NETWORKS	Exact meaning of "Networks"	• TBD • TBD • TBD	• N-1 • N-2 • N-3	• LOC • LOC • LOC	• TITLE • TITLE • TITLE
DATA	Exact meaning of "Data"	• TBD • TBD • TBD	• DA-1 • DA-2 • DA-3	• LOC • LOC • LOC	• TITLE • TITLE • TITLE
USERS	Exact meaning of "Users"	• TBD • TBD • TBD	• U-1 • U-2 • U-3	• LOC • LOC • LOC	• TITLE • TITLE • TITLE

Figure 4-19. *Asset inventory (location and owner)*

With the end of the year coming quickly, the teams transferred their now complete and accurate inventory into their chosen tool for a CMDB. As they were transferring this information, the teams also set up quick self-service tickets for asset owners to manage their assets quickly and easily throughout their life cycle. The workflows were completed for all asset classes to manage them accurately and efficiently throughout their very different life cycle phases. The last step in the process was deploying a tool to perform asset discovery and automate their additions or modifications in the CMDB.

Overall, the company continued to properly use and manage its CMDB. While reactive to implementing and going through an asset management program, the company will be proactive in any future incidents they encounter. And, as a bonus, the team learned a few key lessons along the way:

- **Structure matters**. Road maps and implementation plans are important for any tool integration, especially with asset management.

- **Tools don't always help**. The tool's first tactic was not successful. While they eventually were able to use the tool, it wasn't until they stopped aiming for perfection and moved to good enough that they started to become successful with asset management.

- **Ownership requires buy-in**. Avoid assigning ownership without getting buy-in from the individuals assigned as asset owners.

Example 3. Data Protection Strategy, Please

A large online insurance carrier was concerned about not having a firm grasp on critical data after experiencing a breach and was the main subject of security news. Management was concerned about the public reputation, and the CISO was concerned that the organization had not prioritized a data protection strategy. Raising data classification to the top of their strategic items, the team consulted with an expert for lessons learned on assigning policies/labels and do's and don'ts.

The team approached the problem by establishing a few key ground rules to help identify critical assets before diving into the actual solutions. These ground rules helped keep the team from falling into pitfalls or stalling due to a hang-up on a less-than-optimal task. The first rule was "the payoff for data security should be greater than the resource investment in data security." The second rule was "security is about protecting the data."

A team of five members from various parts of the organization was formed to define critical data/crown jewels. Following the first ground rule, they decided to focus on identifying the most critical data for tracking. This meant they would not track every data set in an inventory system (or worksheet) with a specific tag. Rather, they would identify the most critical data based on priority and then inventory the high priority, leaving the lower-priority assets for later capture.

Using one definition, they started by identifying risk to level-set on what was meant by risk to everyone. NISTIR 7621r1 offered a great risk framework definition that fit their organization:

$$(\text{Threats} + \text{Vulnerabilities}) + \text{Likelihood} = \text{Impact}.$$

For ease, clarity, and alignment to the insurance industry, they settled on the NISTIR 7621r1 definition, keeping likelihood as they found a way to apply actuarial methods to help inform probability.[30] The execution read something like "Risk is a function of threats, vulnerabilities, the likelihood of an event, and the potential impact such an event would have on the company."[31]

Next, they walked through the tedious task of identifying what data they had and then defining the organization's impact. They used an asset inventory worksheet to categorize the data asset and assign a data tag.

Next, the team set out to define what was critical and non-critical data. Eventually, they agreed on the "crown jewels" definition and measures. They created organizational data definitions and standards as an output from this process—for example, a US Social Security number formatted as ######### (as opposed to ###-##-####), which helped ensure no other number formats used this representation (e.g., account numbers, customer numbers, invoice numbers).

---

[30] The formula is now proprietary to the company.
[31] Borrowed from the NISTIR 7621r1 definition.

The NISTIR 7621r1 method identified and prioritized data types through a high/medium/low. While taking this approach, they stumbled upon a common problem in many organizations: vast amounts of unknown and unstructured data objects (documents, sheets, presentations, etc.) with potential crown jewels or copies outside of known data stores. This stalled the effort slightly, as the scope widened from a known location to a large set of unknown sources. With the help of the outside consultant, automated scanning tools were used to complete the identification and classification of objects. The effort regained some momentum, although with a much wider data location scope, and the team could move on to inventorying the high-priority data assets.

The team used a worksheet to capture the data inventory, proper tagging, and last known location based on the agreed-to definitions. This approach was less of a drain on resources. It functioned as a high-priority top-down view rather than a bottom-up view of the full data set to identify information classified and labeled according to a standardized data classification scheme.

With this in place, the team could now manage the risk to these data assets by (later) putting controls in place to protect the data. Overall, the organization defined their top critical data assets, which set them up nicely to manage in a CMDB. The managers and executives now grasped their critical data assets and better understood what was truly at risk. And, as a bonus, the team learned a few key lessons along the way:

- **Definitions matter.** Do not categorize critical data without first defining what the organization means by what's *at risk*. Also, do not categorize critical data without defining *critical* (e.g., high impact, medium impact, low impact). The teams need definitions well before identifying the data and creating the data inventory.

- **Take one bite at a time**. Do not define each data set with a specific tag. The critical data effort can start with the most critical data (i.e., crown jewels) as the highest priority, and then the lower-priority data assets can be inventoried and investigated.

- **Optimize resources**. Do not spend much time on areas that will have little impact. The overall organizational payoff for data security should be greater than the time and people invested.

Example 4. What Risk?

An original equipment manufacturer in the US auto industry was struggling to understand the cyber risk to the organization. The organizational culture was that parts were made on the assembly line, and they had no critical assets worth cyber protection. The company could not understand the risk.

The main challenge was the existence of various viewpoints on what was at risk. Many people in the organization felt that the data on computers was at risk, but that did not impact the assembly line or the production of the parts.

One manager, worried about the networked connection between the assembly line and the computers in the office, introduced this as a possible problem worth investigating. This particular manager hired a cybersecurity consultant to help bring together these individual viewpoints of the risk problem.

A quick walk-through of the risk functions made clear the connection between the office computers (i.e., information technology) and the assembly line (i.e., operational technology) introduced risk, as illustrated in Figure 4-20.

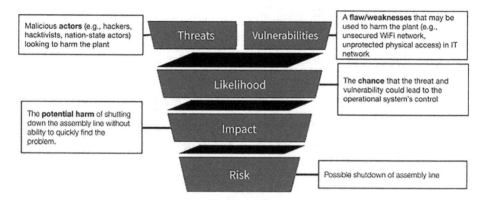

Figure 4-20. Application of the risk definition

The collectively defined business impact of an IT incident that could lead to an assembly line incident helped the organization understand the risk. From that point on, communication of cybersecurity risk became wildly easier throughout the plant and the organization.

Pitfalls to Avoid

Spending time exploring and defining the real risk is not without challenges. Avoiding pitfalls can help move the organization toward understanding the real risk.

The following are common pitfalls to avoid:

- **Pitfall 1**: Having more than one approach to defining critical assets. Multiple approaches with multiple definitions will inevitably create conflict. Definition crumbles, and data object classifications result from more than one approach to defining critical assets while taking critical resources away from the key problem: managing the security of the critical assets.

- **Pitfall 2**: Merging what you think is critical vs. what an attacker is after. When organizations fall into this trap, the clear prioritization of programs and activities becomes overwhelming. It distracts from what is critical, pointing this important effort toward a major pitfall: trying to protect everything. Organizations that fall into this trap are at risk of living up to the short, pithy saying that to protect everything is to protect nothing.

- **Pitfall 3**: Defining critical assets too broadly. Organizations that do not level-set on the appropriate criticality definition, largely based on industry standards, regulations, or peer-group use, fall into the too-broad category—leading to a less-than-crisp understanding of what is most valuable to the organization.

CHAPTER 5

Manage the Problem

Introduction

With the core problem understood, establishing and managing a cyber risk program becomes infinitely more focused and effective. Bring management into focus with a known framework (as a guide, not a solution), structure the management approach in accordance with the program, and set a review cadence to ensure your management approach remains relevant.

With time invested in exploring and categorizing crucial organizational assets and a crisp cybersecurity goal articulated, the problem being solved is, at the very least, understood: cybersecurity risk to critical assets. Now, managing[1] that cybersecurity risk has a better chance for success than managing without a clear understanding of the problem.

Organizations can certainly struggle with even the most basic steps in starting a cybersecurity risk management program. There is pressure from the oversight level to demonstrate and articulate how the risk is being addressed. There is pressure from the executive level to demonstrate a clear mitigation strategy for the cybersecurity risks known within the organization. There is pressure from the top management level to prioritize, resource, and complete planned initiatives. There is pressure

---

[1] Keep in mind that managing the risk provides a clear path for measuring the successful management of cybersecurity risk as well, since the "what you are measuring" needs to be clear before measuring. Successful management relies heavily on feedback metrics, so the next chapter covers the specifics on "how to measure."

© Ryan Leirvik 2023
R. Leirvik, *Understand, Manage, and Measure Cyber Risk*,
https://doi.org/10.1007/978-1-4842-9319-5_5

from the middle management level to demonstrate clear progress on stated goals. There is pressure from all levels of engineering to get the problem solved appropriately (i.e., not just for the satisfaction of executives or managers). There is pressure from within to discover and prevent what an attacker may target next. The one typically bridled with this pressure? The chief information security officer.

The simple fact that cybersecurity is still fairly new and examples of how best to manage it are also new exacerbates this pressure. Each of the levels mentioned earlier can have varying degrees of experience on successful cybersecurity programs. As experience progresses, so does this understanding of the problem and the relevant programs that help. This means that the best practice for managing an overall cybersecurity program has not yet been established. Each person at each level offers differing insights into how best to solve the problem the way they understand it. This is typically where management approaches clash and where the added pressure of politics enters; which particular party of ideas is the one not to upset?[2]

The starting point here is to focus on the overall program before jumping into managing each risk or each category of risks. Some simple rules exist when it comes to establishing a program:

- Focus on one framework to start.

- Structure the management approach along the program framework.

- Set a review frequency for the overall program.

- Prepare to respond and recover from an event, as part of the program.

---

[2] Arguably, in faultless organizations, the solution that best solves the problem is the focus, reducing the need to consider the swaying influence of those who have achieved power with the organization. Many organizations are not faultless, so the conduct of politics is a consideration when solving how best to manage cybersecurity risk.

Details and helpful tools around these rules are broadened later in the chapter. But first, here are some general observations and guidelines around managing cybersecurity risk in any organization.

General Observations and Guidelines for Managing the Risk

Before diving into the rules for establishing a program and then managing the risk, an appreciation for some general cyber risk management observations and guidelines is best established up front.

Observations

First, every organization organizes itself differently. No one organization is the same as another.[3] Although corporate structure, titles, and management approaches may be similar within industries, each organization operates differently. This individual, organizational uniqueness challenges any standard program structure for cybersecurity risk management. How an organization is organized extends into how specific technology deployment management decisions are made to support the overall organizational mission.

Second, each organization deploys technology differently. No one deployment matches exactly any other[4] deployment. Although service

---

[3] Many factors lead to why technology deployments differ, from mission to technical fabric to people. From the technical side, almost no organizational tech stack matches another. But more importantly, technology is typically deployed by humans, and from the human resources side, each organization has different people, and each person follows processes slightly differently. And these impact deployments more than any independent organizational mission.

[4] Contrary to some belief, cloud deployments fall well into the category of "no one deployment is quite the same as another."

providers and programs may be similar in many organizations, the actual design, deployment, testing, monitoring, and use of the technology always differs within each organization. This uniqueness in technology configuration challenges any cybersecurity risk management program as protecting critical assets can be different in all environments.

Third, every organization is at a different level of cybersecurity maturity. And without a well-defined program, measuring against peers cannot be practically comparable.

Guidelines

Based on the observations, a few general guidelines exist for implementing a cybersecurity risk management program.

First, a "quick win" may be achieved for any organization by settling on one known cyber risk management approach (i.e., a common framework or standard) for a program that best fits the organizational mission. The chosen approach does not need to be, and should not be, *the only* way cybersecurity is managed—no single framework fits any organization's risk profile perfectly—but one single known approach can function as a starting point and be modified as the cyber risk management program matures. Starting with a published framework to guide the program provides a structure that is helpful when aligning cybersecurity activities and outcomes to business objectives, using easy-to-understand-and-explain cybersecurity concepts that are immediately useful in any organization.

Second, following a published framework helps create a common language for an organization around cybersecurity activities and management. A common vernacular is tremendously helpful in facilitating dialogue around common themes in cybersecurity risk management, such as threats, vulnerabilities, impact, and risk.

For example, in the United States, the National Institute of Standards and Technology (NIST) released the first version (i.e., version 1.0) of the Framework for Improving Critical Infrastructure Cybersecurity (CSF) on February 12, 2014. This framework acts as a structured way to help understand and address cybersecurity risks faced by any organization, not just critical infrastructure. This CSF provides a core set of activities and outcomes that may be used to determine a cybersecurity program's current state.[5] In the United States, using a framework such as the CSF as the starting point of a cybersecurity program can provide both a dialect and a known structure across industries and regulators.

Another example, starting in the United Kingdom and later adopted by international standards organizations, the International Organization for Standardization (ISO) and the International Electrotechnical Commission (IEC) released the ISO/IEC 27001 on October 15, 2005, as a set of controls for information security management as part of the ISO/IEC 27K series. Starting with well-known and available standards, like those in the ISO/IEC 27K series, can help address one of the biggest challenges organizations face in both design and communication. Adopting a known standard can communicate cybersecurity activities in clear ways to managers and engineers within the organization, as well as to others outside the organization, such as regulators, auditors, and oversight executives.

Third, organizations may address risk quickly by assigning clear management roles, such as security adversary roles and supervisory roles, to categorical cybersecurity risks. Every cybersecurity challenge has a person at the center of the problem that someone is trying to manage. Even the adversary has a person at the center of the objective.[6] Inviting

---

[5] The current state as well as the future state and activities are highly customizable and may be directly aligned to organizational objectives.

[6] At least for now. Automation continues to increase, but even automation still needs a person at some point of the process.

others into the problem can help shed light on other relevant factors within the organization, such as activities, behaviors, opposing incentives, and individuals who may help during an incident. One method that works when inviting others into the problem: Cast a wide net and align to one way of addressing the risk.

Fourth, always be prepared to respond. Preparing for a cyber incident takes foresight and planning, and responding to a cyber incident takes internal coordination and efficiency. The lack of either preparation or execution can quickly increase the incident severity and overall risk to the organization.

With these general program observations and guidelines established, diving into the rules has a bit more context.

Rules to Follow

Simplifying how risk is managed is no easy task in any organization, but some rules exist to help set proper conditions for establishing a cybersecurity program.

RULES TO FOLLOW: MANAGING THE PROBLEM

TAKEAWAYS

Four basic rules in managing cybersecurity risk.

- **Rule 1**: Focus on one framework
- **Rule 2**: Structure the program approach
- **Rule 3**: Set a program review frequency
- **Rule 4**: Prepare to respond (... and recover)

Focus on One Framework

How an organization addresses cybersecurity is critical when it comes to reducing overall risk and mitigating the severity of any cyber incident. This means having an established, structured approach for the whole of the cybersecurity program, that is, a scaffolding for ensuring the program itself is broad enough to address the risks and a prescribed guide for the way each risk is addressed.

Enter the framework: a structured way to address cyber risk program management, helping understand and address cybersecurity risks faced by the organization. With a framework, appropriate cyber risk management may effortlessly combine the concepts of critical asset management and organizational preparedness to respond, offering one risk management approach for mitigating cyber risk. However, the complication with frameworks is that no one framework fits any one organization's risk profile perfectly.[7] So frameworks may act best as a starting point but must be modified over time as organizational cyber risk management matures within the overall program.

Many well-defined, highly useful frameworks manage risk for an entire organization or enterprise. Enterprise risk management (ERM) is a defined market category for organizations to anticipate, estimate, and address risk to the entire organization. The Enterprise Risk Management—Integrated Framework[8] by COSO adds the ability to define and manage the uncertainty that may erode enterprise value. ERM, however, is not the circumscribed focus for this portion of managing cyber risk. It is the overarching function in which cybersecurity risk management must fit, requiring consideration when choosing the right cybersecurity risk management framework.

In general, available cybersecurity management frameworks come in many shapes and sizes. That is, frameworks available today each address certain risks at various organizational levels. For example, program frameworks, like the NIST CSF and ISO 27001, address the overall state

---

[7] Mentioned in the section "Guidelines," this is worth repeating.

[8] The Committee of Sponsoring Organizations of the Treadway Commission, Enterprise Risk Management—Integrated Framework, 1985–2021. More information is at www.coso.org.

of a cybersecurity program. Frameworks like the NIST SP 800-53 and CIS
Critical Security Controls address technical and administrative controls
for functionality and assurance across diverse requirements. And overall
risk frameworks, like the NIST SP 800-37/RMF (NIST RMF) and ISO 27005,
address overall risk.

Several cybersecurity program frameworks exist, including the
following:

- The **NIST CSF** is a structure for approaching a
  cybersecurity program. Originally intended for
  critical infrastructure, it has grown in popularity and
  application across all industries in the United States.
  The CSF may easily complement or work well with
  other programs.

- **ISO/IEC 27001** is an international system or standard
  for the security management of a system. It may
  be used as an overall framework for other InfoSec
  approaches, and certification is offered (as well as other
  parts of the ISO/IEC 27K series).

Several risk management frameworks exist, including the following:

- The **NIST RMF** is a risk management framework for the
  enterprise and intended to outline key activities, largely
  for the US government. It may be used to frame and
  apply key NIST/FIPS standards.

- **ISO/IEC 27005** is a process for risk management.

Several control frameworks exist, such as the following:

- The **NIST SP 800-53**[9] provides a categorical and systematic list of security and privacy controls. A requirement for the US government and its contractors, any organization may adopt and adapt the recommended controls in almost any risk management process.

- **CIS Critical Security Controls**[10] provides safeguards for activities to help focus security efforts.

Other frameworks include the Factor Analysis of Information Risk (FAIR) framework, the NIST 800 Series, MITRE ATT&CK, and many others. Categorical collections of risks exist for specific domain areas, like the Open Worldwide Application Security Project® (OWASP).[11]

Beginning with a known framework is a helpful guide in shaping a program to best understand the risks faced by an organization and positioning the organization to speak a common language across multiple industries and sectors. To concretely set cybersecurity risk management concepts as a *program* and provide illustrative examples of framework deployment for cyber risk program control, the CSF is the framework used going forward.

As mentioned previously, the NIST released version 1.0 of the CSF in early 2014, released version 1.1 in mid-2018, and plans to release 2.0 in late 2024.[12] The CSF acts as a structured way to help understand and address cybersecurity risks faced by any organization, not just critical

---

[9] Check the latest version available at https://csrc.nist.gov/publications/detail/sp/800-53/rev-5/final/.

[10] CIS Critical Security Controls is a registered trademark. Check the latest version available at www.cisecurity.org/controls/.

[11] The Open Worldwide Application Security Project® is a registered trademark. The OWASP foundation is a nonprofit focused on software security. The latest information may be found at https://owasp.org.

[12] Version 2.0 will include a new "Govern" function to the current five functions, to "emphasize cybersecurity risk management governance outcomes" according to the NIST.

infrastructure. Adoption of the CSF is increasing in many US industries, from retail to banking to insurance to energy and the government.[13]

Starting a cybersecurity risk management program based on the CSF is a helpful way to quickly understand the risks faced by an organization and position the organization to speak a common language across multiple industries and sectors. Using the CSF can provide a quick win to guide technology deployment and build in-depth defenses.

In short, the CSF aims to reduce and better manage[14] cybersecurity risks across any organizational size (e.g., small business, large business, enterprise) and industry (e.g., hospitality, banking, finance, energy, retail). The CSF offers five functions: Identify, Protect, Detect, Respond, and Recover. Figure 5-1 provides a high-level overview of the CSF as an introduction.

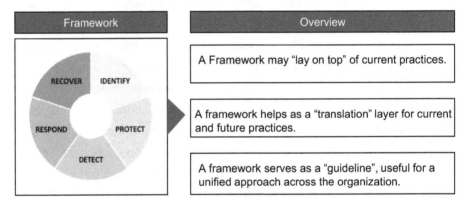

Figure 5-1. *A high-level introductory overview of the CSF*

It is not a miscalculation that *Identify* is at the top of the list. It is not a mistake that *understanding* the technology used in the organization is the starting point for understanding, managing, and measuring

---

[13] Note that the use of the CSF is voluntary for the private sector, but is not optional for the US government.

[14] From the NIST, "[t]hough the Cybersecurity Framework is not a one-size-fits-all approach to managing cybersecurity risk for organizations, it is ultimately aimed at reducing and better managing these risks." www.nist.gov/cyberframework/.

cybersecurity risk. By leading off with *Identify*, the CSF points out that when understanding deployed technology, the risk is the starting point. This attention to risk drives what to measure, how to inform your strategy, how much to invest in a program, and other program-related components. At this point, it should make sense why understanding[15] the risk comes before managing and measuring.

Before implementing any chosen approach, it is necessary to familiarize the approach's goals and use. As the CSF is the chosen approach for the illustrations and examples going forward, it may be worthwhile to visit the NIST website[16] for detailed information sufficient to move forward. The ambition should be to gain familiarization with the use of the CSF in introducing certain standards, guidelines, and best practices to properly establish a program for managing cybersecurity risk.

Structure the Program Approach

Structure matters. Purposely arranging the specific parts of a cybersecurity program, with clear relationships between the parts, constructs a program sufficient to address the risk complexities the program is asked to address.

Structure is the essential factor for getting things done in a proper cybersecurity program. Having a proper structure keeps the organization focused on the risk, applying critical resources to the top problems so they may be managed and tracked and setting a platform for reporting to the board.[17] A proper structure helps keep teams focused on what is most important, maintaining attention on response and recovery when engrossment around the next best protection tool arrives—the shiny

---

[15] "A problem thoroughly understood is always fairly simple." Charles Kettering was quoted as saying in the book *Dynamic Work Simplification* (1971) by W. Clements Zinck, p. 122.

[16] See the NIST CSF at www.nist.gov/cyberframework/new-framework/.

[17] See Chapter 9.

object that typically takes critical attention away from the border risk. A proper structure helps ensure the broadest possible areas have attention, providing guardianship over typically neglected areas that attackers use when they notice no one is paying attention.

Structure is not easy, though. Properly anticipating, categorizing, and arranging the core elements is hard to get accurate each time. Some resist structure, while others hold on to unproven and ineffective structures. The benefit of choosing a known program structure bypasses the step of trying to properly determine all the appropriate pieces. It borrows from individuals in the field who have a deeper understanding of the problem. Additional benefits of choosing a known program structure include immediately aligning organizational reporting to key objectives. And, once that is complete, the problem of structuring and managing is half solved.[18]

To get started on setting and following a structure, some steps exist to follow when implementing a program framework, the CSF in this case, for cybersecurity risk management.

How to Structure the Approach

To begin structuring the approach to cybersecurity program management, take the following steps:

- **Step 1.** Set the structure.

- **Step 2.** Align risk-mitigating activities.

- **Step 3.** Assign roles and responsibilities.

- **Step 4.** Identify gaps and the appropriate activities to fill them.

---

[18] A well-defined problem is half solved. Some variation of this quote is usually attributed to Charles Kettering.

- **Step 5.** Look externally (third-party risk management [TPRM]).

- **Step 6.** Pick the right tools and avoid distraction.

Step 1. Set the Structure

Starting a cybersecurity program can be a daunting task. Even after trying a variety of risk frameworks to get a full grip on risk management, recalibrating the organization to a new program or way of viewing a program can be equally daunting. This is where a program framework like the CSF can help.

Understanding the CSF and its purpose, any organization can get started with the framework's full version[19] or a simplified version.[20]

First, a simplified version of the CSF may be used in a system or worksheet. Figure 5-2 illustrates a starting point as an example. The objective here is to become familiarized with the core functions, what they mean to cybersecurity risk management, and the associated activities that typically fit within each category. The functions are mutually exclusive. Building awareness of what organizational cybersecurity activity fits within which function helps set the foundation for the structure to work properly in covering a broad range of cybersecurity risks.

---

[19] The full CSF and supporting documents are at www.nist.gov/cyberframework.
[20] Note the descriptions and activities used to go forward are modified for simplicity. Turns out this modification has worked as a simplified way to "get started" in any organization looking to begin quickly and sufficiently using, and socializing, the CSF.

FUNCTION	DESCRIPTION	ACTIVITIES
IDENTIFY	Know the most critical assets	• Asset Management • Business Environment • Governance • Risk Assessment/ Strategy
PROTECT	Establish meaningful safeguards and behaviors around most critical information	• Access Control • Awareness and Training • Data Security • Information Protection • Maintenance • Protective Technology
DETECT	Monitor for and discover potential cybersecurity events	• Anomalies and Events • Continuous Monitoring • Detection Processes
RESPOND	Prepare for and mitigate cybersecurity events	• Response Planning • Communications (internal and external) • Analysis • Mitigation • Improvements (response)
RECOVER	Reduce the impact and maximize recovery time	• Recovery planning • Improvements (recovery) • Communications (internal and external)

Figure 5-2. *An example of a simplified version of the CSF used to get started*

Second, with each function understood and properly described, a risk management approach may be built off this point as a good start for the entire organization. This includes choosing the appropriate activities to plan, such as the activities proposed to address risk in each category, and completing each function's activities. (The Activities section is removed to provide for the proposed activities needed with the organization.) Figure 5-3 illustrates the type of worksheet that may be used. For example, if the broad goal in the Identify function is to know the most critical assets, what activities are needed to get there that require approval? Consider, for instance, a complete asset management capability. This activity would become a proposed activity, as it aligns with the overall goal but is not necessarily in progress now. As the proposed activities are selected, a basis for an activity road map, or plan, begins to take shape.

FUNCTION	DESCRIPTION	PROPOSED ACTIVITIES
IDENTIFY	Know the most critical assets	• <Proposed activity> • <Proposed activity> • <Proposed activity>
PROTECT	Establish meaningful safeguards and behaviors around most critical information	• <Proposed activity> • <Proposed activity> • <Proposed activity>
DETECT	Monitor for and discover potential cybersecurity events	• <Proposed activity> • <Proposed activity> • <Proposed activity>
RESPOND	Prepare for and mitigate cybersecurity events	• <Proposed activity> • <Proposed activity> • <Proposed activity>
RECOVER	Reduce the impact and maximize recovery time	• <Proposed activity> • <Proposed activity> • <Proposed activity>

Figure 5-3. *Worksheet with proposed activities to functions*

Step 2. Align the Risk-Mitigating Activities

With the mapping of proposed activities needed to address the spirit of the function, current cybersecurity activities (current activities) in progress may be added. The goal here is to visualize the difference between the activities needed or planned (i.e., proposed activities) and the current activities that have already begun. With a side-by-side comparison, the gaps between where the organization is not and where it needs to go begin to materialize. (Note: More on this in a later step.)

First, collect the current activities in progress within the organization. This includes all cybersecurity-related initiatives, programs, or efforts. Each current activity or effort should fall into only one function. Recall that the functions are mutually exclusive. Figure 5-4 presents the worksheet expanded to capture these activities.

FUNCTION	DESCRIPTION	PROPOSED ACTIVITIES	CURRENT ACTIVITIES
IDENTIFY	Know the most critical assets	• \<Proposed activity\> • \<Proposed activity\> • \<Proposed activity\>	• \<Activity in progress\> • \<Activity in progress\> • \<Activity in progress\>
PROTECT	Establish meaningful safeguards and behaviors around most critical information	• \<Proposed activity\> • \<Proposed activity\> • \<Proposed activity\>	• \<Activity in progress\> • \<Activity in progress\> • \<Activity in progress\>
DETECT	Monitor for and discover potential cybersecurity events	• \<Proposed activity\> • \<Proposed activity\> • \<Proposed activity\>	• \<Activity in progress\> • \<Activity in progress\> • \<Activity in progress\>
RESPOND	Prepare for and mitigate cybersecurity events	• \<Proposed activity\> • \<Proposed activity\> • \<Proposed activity\>	• \<Activity in progress\> • \<Activity in progress\> • \<Activity in progress\>
RECOVER	Reduce the impact and maximize recovery time	• \<Proposed activity\> • \<Proposed activity\> • \<Proposed activity\>	• \<Activity in progress\> • \<Activity in progress\> • \<Activity in progress\>

Figure 5-4. *Worksheet with current activities added*

Here, a timeline of the activities has been informally introduced as part of the activities needed for the program. If the proposed activities are approved within the organization, a timeline may be added to when they begin. These proposed activities become the next effort to begin once the current activities are completed. With the appropriate framework function filled out with activities, a structured view of your current organizational approach emerges.

Step 3. Assign Roles and Responsibilities

Managers, get ready to dig in. This is where the structure begins to lean toward managing the program.

As with any good program management, individual responsibility is a key component of successfully managing cybersecurity. And one success factor to focus on here is the activity lead: that is, someone to take the lead on and responsibility for each risk mitigation initiative.

First, assign activity responsibility to the respective activity. Responsibility should be assigned for each activity within each function. Use the position title (e.g., lead developer, head of physical security) over individual names, as people tend to change more frequently than titles during the span of a cybersecurity program. However, assigning the title with a corresponding name of the incumbent allows for increased personal responsibility and the ability to quickly identify the individual responsible for the activity. Figure 5-5 presents the worksheet expanded to capture responsibility for the listed activities.

FUNCTION	DESCRIPTION	PROPOSED ACTIVITIES	CURRENT ACTIVITIES	RESPONSIBILITY
IDENTIFY	Know the most critical assets	• <Proposed activity> • <Proposed activity> • <Proposed activity>	• <Activity in progress> • <Activity in progress> • <Activity in progress>	• <Title, Name> • <Title, Name> • <Title, Name>
PROTECT	Establish meaningful safeguards and behaviors around most critical information	• <Proposed activity> • <Proposed activity> • <Proposed activity>	• <Activity in progress> • <Activity in progress> • <Activity in progress>	• <Title, Name> • <Title, Name> • <Title, Name>
DETECT	Monitor for and discover potential cybersecurity events	• <Proposed activity> • <Proposed activity> • <Proposed activity>	• <Activity in progress> • <Activity in progress> • <Activity in progress>	• <Title, Name> • <Title, Name> • <Title, Name>
RESPOND	Prepare for and mitigate cybersecurity events	• <Proposed activity> • <Proposed activity> • <Proposed activity>	• <Activity in progress> • <Activity in progress> • <Activity in progress>	• <Title, Name> • <Title, Name> • <Title, Name>
RECOVER	Reduce the impact and maximize recovery time	• <Proposed activity> • <Proposed activity> • <Proposed activity>	• <Activity in progress> • <Activity in progress> • <Activity in progress>	• <Title, Name> • <Title, Name> • <Title, Name>

Figure 5-5. *Worksheet with proposed responsibilities, by title and name, assigned to activities*

With global or disparate teams, assigning roles is critical. The organization's defensive posture can look good on paper, but a person must implement it and own its success (or failure).

Second, assign a due date for each activity. Assigning the due date provides a sense of planning for the completion of the activity. Due dates are a helpful data point to provide expected maturity for specific activities and program dependencies. For example, knowing the asset management program will be complete in June informs that a dependent program, like a data loss prevention for identified critical data, may begin in July. Figure 5-6 presents the worksheet expanded to capture due dates for listed activities.

FUNCTION	DESCRIPTION	PROPOSED ACTIVITIES	CURRENT ACTIVITIES	RESPONSIBILITY	DUE DATE
IDENTIFY	Know the most critical assets	• <Proposed activity> • <Proposed activity> • <Proposed activity>	• <Activity in progress> • <Activity in progress> • <Activity in progress>	• <Title, Name> • <Title, Name> • <Title, Name>	• <Date> • <Date> • <Date>
PROTECT	Establish meaningful safeguards and behaviors around most critical information	• <Proposed activity> • <Proposed activity> • <Proposed activity>	• <Activity in progress> • <Activity in progress> • <Activity in progress>	• <Title, Name> • <Title, Name> • <Title, Name>	• <Date> • <Date> • <Date>
DETECT	Monitor for and discover potential cybersecurity events	• <Proposed activity> • <Proposed activity> • <Proposed activity>	• <Activity in progress> • <Activity in progress> • <Activity in progress>	• <Title, Name> • <Title, Name>	• <Date> • <Date>
RESPOND	Prepare for and mitigate cybersecurity events	• <Proposed activity> • <Proposed activity> • <Proposed activity>	• <Activity in progress> • <Activity in progress> • <Activity in progress>	• <Title, Name> • <Title, Name> • <Title, Name>	• <Date> • <Date> • <Date>
RECOVER	Reduce the impact and maximize recovery time	• <Proposed activity> • <Proposed activity> • <Proposed activity>	• <Activity in progress> • <Activity in progress> • <Activity in progress>	• <Title, Name> • <Title, Name> • <Title, Name>	• <Date> • <Date> • <Date>

Figure 5-6. *Worksheet with due dates for listed activities*

Assigning titles and dates to initiatives has the added benefit of demonstrating resource constraints. Initiatives without assignments illustrate potential gaps in the security team. Titles with too many initiatives illustrate overloaded positions in the security team and a potential single point of failure should the person not be available for work suddenly (e.g., leave, fall ill, care for a family member). Overall, assigning roles ensures that the ownership and management of activity are in place so that risk is not lost.

Step 4. Identify Gaps and the Appropriate Activities to Fill Them

The difference between the proposed activities and the current activities displays gaps and provides an opportunity to quickly view the possible weaknesses in the current organizational approach to cybersecurity. Identifying these gaps and selecting the appropriate activities to fill them provides a road map for action to take in the future.

First, look at the titles and names assigned to the activities. Do the people assigned to these activities have the appropriate skills or knowledge to complete the activities? For example, is there a cloud security team member assigned to non-cloud activities? Are there too many system administrators assigned to non–system admin activities? How many security team members are assigned to general IT activities, like asset management? Is the role for servicing a machine on a cloud provider (e.g., AWS, Azure) lacking cloud architecture and monitoring skills?

In some cases, a specialized security engineer is a clear lead for an activity. In other cases, general IT engineers may own tasks. Looking for and teasing out the resource gaps might help free up security resources or make a case for more.

The other way to look at it is through optimization. Do some activities have similar conjoining underpinnings? Could the same role handle these types of activities, for example, data integrity? The same role assigned to asset management may be the same role assigned to access control.

One of the gaps may be too many engineers and not enough leaders across the organizational business units. Is there a need to look to a *business information security officer* (BISO)—a senior leader in a business unit responsible for the practice and alignment of security, someone responsible for visibility and operational security posture of the business unit, working and collaborating cross-functionally across business units and up to the chief information security officer (CISO)? A look at the program as it stands may help identify these types of resource gaps.

Second, look at the activities separately. Are there gaps in the program? Is there too much emphasis on vulnerability management but not enough on insider risk? Did security architecture lose out to threat assessments with the push to cloud services? A look at the program as it stands may help identify these types of activity, or initiative, gaps.

Finally, as a bonus, identify if the appropriate part of the organization owns the program. Building off a program framework can help solidify ownership of the overall program and responsibilities within the organization. Many organizations struggle with full ownership of a cybersecurity program. Whom does it belong to? The CISO? The chief risk officer (CRO)? The chief information officer (CIO)? These types of organizational structure and the actual operating model should be determined before moving forward with the full establishment of the program.

Organizational operating structure varies from organization to organization. The key is to have a clear information security risk owner (e.g., CISO, CRO, information security manager), where organizational incentives are established to maintain risk mitigation solutions. Figure 5-7 illustrates an example where the CISO organization is responsible for the program.

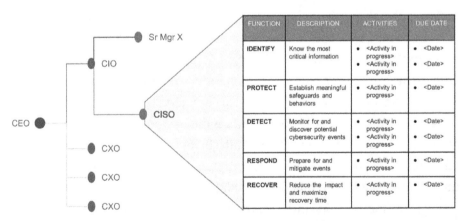

Figure 5-7. *Sample organizational structure with the cybersecurity risk program under the CISO*

With the introduction of the program and internal processes to maintain proper management of the activities, it's time to look outside the organization for risks.

Step 5. Look Externally (Third-Party Risk Management)

Anticipating areas of organizational cybersecurity risk stretches beyond simply internal processes. An individual or an organization that is not part of your organization (referred to as a third party)[21] introduces their own set of risks that can sometimes go overlooked.

External risks, such as outsourced entities, require security attention that expands beyond the primary organizational boundaries to external parties for investigating possible vulnerabilities that may impact the primary organization. This is the essence of third-party risk management (TPRM). The goal is to perform risk management successfully enough to anticipate and remediate issues resulting from the outside party *before* a weakness in that third party is exploited that impacts the organization.

There are many ways to go about managing third-party risk. One solution begins with establishing a formal TPRM program within the organization. Programs like these always best start by gaining internal buy-in from teams who have a stake in the outcome and the management, like governance, risk, and compliance (GRC), overall organizational risk management, cybersecurity, procurement or purchasing, and legal.

---

[21] Also known as *third parties* or *third-party vendors*. These are not the unbiased observers or mediators between two parties. In cybersecurity, these are established relationships between the organization and an outside entity, typically to perform some function the organization wishes to outsource. The 2013 Target Corporation breach is one of the first most notable examples that introduced third-party risk management to the broader public, as well as the boards of directors.

Making a concerted effort to bring in team members early helps prevent internal teams from engaging external third-party vendors without engaging in a TPRM risk identification process.

One simple way to begin a risk management process focused on third parties is to align on what risks are important. One way to do this is to dedicate or hire full-time employees[22] at the onset. Depending upon the depth of any existing third-party risk management program, a dedicated specific team or employee is best. TPRM requires a lot of time and work to properly manage. Assessors of risk stay busy with a wide variety of outside entities or people requiring assessments. For example, dedicated third-party assessors have to retroactively assess the current vendors prior to assessing any new/additional vendors the organization is looking to engage. This process can become a mammoth task, depending on the organization's size, use of outside contractors, and any current backlogs of assessments to complete.

With an identified team or person dedicated to the effort, establish a third-party risk management questionnaire. Regardless of the maturity of a TPRM process, the questionnaire is a strong place to start as support to any current program or to ease future assessments. The questionnaire is established to clarify which areas of risk to probe when considering engagement with an outside party. As with any strong risk management program, choosing one framework as the basis for this questionnaire helps ensure the program has structure.

Continuing with the CSF, a questionnaire may be built around the organization's management process to help with coverage and alignment back to organizational risks; too many frameworks cause alignment problems. At the very basic level, aligning to the CSF may help establish high-level questions for vendor assessment. For example, Figure 5-8 illustrates at least one question per function to begin asking TPRM questions.

---

[22] Ironically, many organizations hire an outside party, like external consultants, to assist with the TPRM effort. These organizations, as well, must undergo a third-party assessment process.

FUNCTION	DESCRIPTION	QUESTION (High Level)
IDENTIFY	Know the most critical information.	What systems or data do they have access to?
PROTECT	Establish meaningful safeguards and behaviors around the most critical information.	What privileged access do they have?
DETECT	Monitor for and discover potential cybersecurity events.	Can they detect anomalous activity?
RESPOND	Prepare for and mitigate cybersecurity events.	Are they prepared to respond?
RECOVER	Reduce the impact and maximize recovery time.	Do they have business continuity and disaster recovery measures in place, if all else fails?

Figure 5-8. *Use of the CSF for TPRM questions*

Understanding each category of the CSF regarding the vendor assists in determining the questions that form the rest of the questionnaire. Not only is it important to assess risks posed to the organization's environment, but also it is important to assess the risk the third party may pose to itself. While this is less important than the former, it is not uncommon to ask questions regarding the vendor's security posture. Some guiding steps may help in this process.

How to Build Out the TPRM Questionnaire

To begin structuring the questionnaire based on the CSF, take the following steps:

- **Step 5a.** Split the TPRM questionnaire into to logical columns.

- **Step 5b.** Build each column upon the one before.

- **Step 5c.** Directly relate the question to the risk.

Step 5a. Split the Questionnaire into Logical Columns

As the construction of the TPRM questionnaire begins, starting with the first function of Identify will help in understanding the problem itself. Questions created in the Identify function assist in building out the rest of the questionnaire.

To get started, split into the following columns: Function (i.e., CSF category), Description (i.e., what the function does), Activities (i.e., CSF subcategories), Requirement Descriptions (i.e., the requirements the subcategory defined), and, arguably the most important, the questions.

Step 5b. Build Each Column Upon the One Before

With the columns split, build each column upon another. To make the questionnaire easier to build out, start with filling in the first four columns and then retroactively return to building out the questions based upon the activities and requirement descriptions.

Step 5c. Directly Relate the Question to the Risk

The questions should be directly related to what the organization is trying to understand, mitigate against, or uncover about the vendor's environment. Let's look at the requirement for Asset Management— ID.AM, which states "... shall maintain an inventory of all the material IT assets and automation system assets supporting the services." The obvious question to ask the vendor here is if they maintain an asset inventory. While that would provide a yes or no answer, it would not give the TPRM assessor enough information to determine the vendor's risk to the organization. When building out questions for the questionnaire, it is best to avoid yes or no questions. Ask questions that require the vendor to go into a bit of detail regarding their process. The requirements of ID.AM-1 and ID.AM-2 ask the following: How do you maintain asset inventory? Is the inventory maintained? This provides your TPRM assessors the ability to understand if the vendor has a handle on their critical assets. Why is this important? If the vendor has a handle on critical assets in a breach event, they can identify, detect, and respond, including alerting third parties (i.e., your organization) of the attack. Figure 5-9 illustrates sample TPRM questions for ID.

FUNCTION	DESCRIPTION	ACTIVITIES	REQUIREMENT (Description)	QUESTION
IDENTIFY	Know your most critical information.	Asset Management (ID.AM)	ID.AM-1 and IDAM-2: Provider shall maintain an inventory of all the material IT assets and automation system assets supporting the services that are in its possession.	1. How do you maintain asset inventory? Is the inventory maintained within an Excel spreadsheet or within a tool? 2. Do you use a tool for asset discovery to maintain a proper listing of all internal and external devices connecting to your network?
		Risk Assessment / Strategy (ID.RA)	ID.RA-1 and ID.RA-6: Provider shall conduct an information security risk assessment on at least an annual basis and manage risks to confidential information and IT systems supporting the services with documented risk management procedures.	1. Does your information security team perform risk assessments at least yearly? 2. What is the process your information security team uses to perform risks assessments? 3. What controls are in place to mitigate risk that arise from the risk assessments?

Figure 5-9. *Sample TPRM questions for ID*

Now that the questionnaire has been established, let's look at more examples for each of the other NIST functions. The Protect function is next on the list. The Protect function determines whether a vendor can properly establish safeguards and behaviors around critical information.

Keep in Mind

The definition for the Protect function is important to note here. The third-party questionnaire asks whether the vendor can establish safeguards around their most critical information. Therefore, it is important to ask very direct questions regarding their access management and their policies to identify risks to their organization. If they know what is critical, they should have no problem establishing protections. If they do not, then protecting what is critical is difficult for the vendor.

Figure 5-10 illustrates TPRM questions for PR.

FUNCTION	DESCRIPTION	ACTIVITIES	REQUIREMENT (Description)	QUESTION
PROTECT	Establish meaningful safeguards and behaviors around the most critical information.	**Identity and Access Control (PR.AC)**	**PR.AC-4:** Provider shall restrict physical and logical access to confidential information and IT systems supporting the services being provided to the minimum level of access and privileges required to perform a function or role.	1. Do you adhere to the principle of least privilege when assigning access to roles? If so, is the policy documented? 2. Which employees and subcontractor roles will have access to <organization's name> data?
		Data Security (PR.DS)	**PR.DS-1, PR.DS-2:** Provider shall encrypt confidential information where possible in storage and in transit.	1. What encryption standard does your organization use? 2. Does customer data leave your production systems under any circumstances? 3. Do you encrypt data at rest? Do you encrypt data in transit?

Figure 5-10. *Sample TPRM questions for PR*

While there are six activity subcategories for the NIST CSF Protect function, the two in Figure 5-10 give a good descriptor of what this function is trying to accomplish. Is the vendor able to properly deploy controls to limit access to only necessary parties, and is your organization's data properly handled when being shared with this vendor? The Protect function is the largest as it spans across many important categories such as Identity and Access Management, Data Security, Awareness and Training, Maintenance, Information Protection, and Protective Technology.

Detect is the next function in the NIST CSF framework. In the context of the TPRM questionnaire, the focus is on a vendor's ability to monitor and discover potential cybersecurity events. This section heavily focuses on the ability of vendors to detect anomalous behavior before it is considered an incident. This type of capability will help your organization identify if this vendor will properly detect any data breach in their environment and subsequently control the risk if detected early enough. Figure 5-11 illustrates TPRM questions for DE.

FUNCTION	DESCRIPTION	ACTIVITIES	REQUIREMENT (Description)	QUESTION
DETECT	Monitor for and discover potential cybersecurity events.	Anomalies and Events (DE.AE)	DE.AE-2: Provider shall analyze security events to identify cyber-attacks and possible attack methods. Provider shall promptly investigate suspected and confirmed attacks and report confirmed attacks related to the services provided under the contractual agreement.	1. Can the vendor detect anomalous activity and events within the environment (i.e., SIEM, proper security controls with alerting)?
		Continuous Monitoring (DE.CM)	DE.CM-1: Provider shall collect and correlate security events from systems and sensors to identify information security incidents and cyber-attacks.	1. How do you log and alert on relevant security events?

Figure 5-11. *Sample TPRM questions for DE*

The Respond function instructs to "prepare for and mitigate cybersecurity events." This section focuses on asking the vendors if they have an incident response program and the regularity at which they test their incident response capabilities within their organization. The most vital point in this section of the questionnaire is to understand the vendor's notification timelines in the event of a security incident/event/breach. Figure 5-12 illustrates TPRM questions for RS.

FUNCTION	DESCRIPTION	ACTIVITIES	REQUIREMENT (Description)	QUESTION
RESPOND	Prepare for and mitigate cybersecurity events.	Response Planning (RS.RP)	RS.RP-1: Provider shall report any confirmed security incidents or data breaches affecting systems or data to <insert organization> promptly and without delay.	1. Do you have formally defined criteria for notifying a client during an incident that might impact the security of their data or systems? What are your SLAs for notification?

Figure 5-12. *Sample TPRM questions for RS*

Finally, the Recover function states "reduce the impact and maximize recovery time." A vendor should focus on recovering and containing any incident. This allows an organization to know if their data was compromised due to a third-party cyber incident. The third party can appropriately manage the risk and has the proper process to stop the damage from getting any worse. Figure 5-13 illustrates TPRM questions for RC.

FUNCTION	DESCRIPTION	ACTIVITIES	REQUIREMENT (Description)	QUESTION
RECOVER	Reduce the impact and maximize recovery time.	**Recovery Planning (RC.RP)**	**RC.RP-1:** Provider shall develop and maintain security recovery plans that are executed during or after an event and restore systems affected by cybersecurity events.	1. What is the cadence for data recovery and testing for integrity within systems?

Figure 5-13. *Illustrates TPRM questions for RC*

The management and use of a third-party questionnaire is extremely important for the success of the third-party risk management program inside your organization. The way your organization decides to deploy the questionnaire (Excel spreadsheet vs. a tool) is less important than the questions you are asking to categorize the overall risk a vendor may present the organization. The ability to understand the risk a third party may pose to your organization, the frequency at which a vendor may need to be reviewed, and the life cycle stage a vendor is in inside the organization allow for the proper management of your cybersecurity program.

Once your questionnaire is complete and deployed in a working process, it may be a good time to verify the value of the vendors in use in your environment.

How to Verify Your External Look

To begin verifying how the company looks to the outside, take the following steps:

- **Step 5d**. Link a Software Bill of Materials (SBOM) to the TPRM program.

- **Step 5e**. Build a risk feedback mechanism for vendors.

- **Step 5f**. Align to procurement and purchasing.

Step 5d. Link a Software Bill of Materials to the TPRM Program

One of the lesser understood challenges in third-party risk, as it applies to the use of software within and by organizations, is the transparency of exactly what is included in software deployed in an organization that is used or purchased from a vendor or outside entity. Software used in most organizations is not typically written by one person or one team, but rather compiled from various software packages and various sources—some new but many reused. Without a clear "content list" of the software components assembled as part of the final software product (used in production), an understanding of what exactly is included in the software package may be quite obfuscated,[23] leaving the full definition of the software and the categories of components largely hidden. A Bill of Materials is used in many mature industries to understand the raw materials (from internal or other sources) that make up a finished product.

---

[23] If this is not immediately shocking, please read (or reread) Chapter 1. Remember, technology is inherently flawed. Compiling components of flawed code within flawed code not only increases the opportunity for vulnerabilities; it also hides those vulnerabilities deep within deployed software.

113

For example, automotive manufacturing, pharmaceuticals, and consumer packaged goods contractually require Bills of Materials as an authoritative source of what is being purchased (received) or sold (shipped). Yet this does not currently exist—in full deployment—for the software industry.[24]

Enter the SBOM—the Software Bill of Materials. An SBOM is a Bill of Materials of software components, outlining the various components and types of components, from other sources, which are used in a final software product. From a risk point of view, an SBOM can be of great assistance when determining the substance of a finished software product. Knowing what components are in deployed software is a primary starting point for the vulnerability management process, especially in assessing the risk of external components from third parties.[25]

Knowing the components of software deployed within an organization provides vulnerability management and software discovery a significant head start, without the need to rely on a vulnerability scanning tool for specific vulnerabilities deployed within the organization or in development. One critical issue within TPRM is the ability to quickly identify organizational exposure to a known software vulnerability. The ability to gather, consume, and use SBOM data provides information and direction that would otherwise consume valuable resources (e.g., time, people, money).

Actual consumption and use of the software materials data, however, is not as easy as it sounds. Reading and using the data in the SBOM will depend first on the format[26] and then on the process to make use of it. For the overall risk program, however, the important consideration is in

---

[24] Ironically, each of the examples used relies heavily on software to do business, like, say, create and print/communicate a Bill of Materials.

[25] Organizations commonly rely on SBOMs for vulnerability discovery (and then management) in non-native code. So, naturally, the SBOM discussion for risk management purposes begins with the common source—external parties.

[26] The format matters. At the time of this writing, two formats were competing as possible standards (CycloneDX and SPDX), among a number of others.

establishing a clear and manageable connection (or link) between the use of the data provided in the SBOM and the practical risk mitigation steps within a TPRM program and the overall vulnerability management program. For an organization struggling to get started, one quick way could be the following.

First, draft a software asset inventory plan that includes the request/ creation, consumption, and use of the data; for a head start, pull from the appropriate section of the chosen risk framework (e.g., ID in the NIST CSF, A.8.1.1./A.8.2.2 in ISO 27001, CM-8 in the NIST SP 800-53). Crisply define three basic action steps needed to use the information within the organization: (1) identify and inventory (in an authoritative source) components and categories/classes (e.g., software component, software service) of relevant software—planning ahead for software that *may be used* in the near term; (2) outline how the components will be assessed for known vulnerabilities (or risk, if impact categories are clear) within the currently deployed, used, or developed software; and (3) clearly define how to manage discovered vulnerabilities, including the documentation of vulnerability mitigation actions, when issues (known vulnerabilities or perceived vulnerabilities) are identified whether internally and across third parties.

Second, test the plan for execution efficiency, starting with the ability to complete the inventory. Expect that the data will take time to digest and that only a fraction of the data will be available in the short term— especially in big programs. Requesting SBOMs, whether existing or not, from third parties can be both challenging and telling in order to perform (or begin performing) vulnerability risk assessments for currently deployed software.[27] (Some third parties may have available SBOMs, and others may not; both say something about the security viewpoint of that particular organization.)

---

[27] This also requires creating SBOMs for in-house software components for vulnerability assessments within internal software development.

Overall, executing the plan is highly dependent upon a few key items: format, process, and ability to digest/action the data. Many organizations get started with a pilot program for one business unit or functional business line, or one application, when figuring out how best to begin. Many times this will mean scanning code repos (internal or third parties, if authorized) for code libraries or software components with known vulnerabilities (e.g., an out-of-date .npm package for a specific .json file). Results from scanning should inform appropriate action according to a remediation plan—forming new insights and revising remediation plans as appropriate management dictates. One helpful tool for vulnerable code in third-party software can be the vendor questionnaire regarding self-described asset inventory processes (see ID.AM-1 and ID.AM-2 in Figure 5-9). Another tool is the legal contract (see the section "Step 5f. Align to Procurement and Purchasing") to determine if a vendor has a legal obligation to handle known vulnerabilities, as part of the overall vulnerability management process. The important part is to have a sufficient approach to managing key dependencies for a risk-informed and efficient program.

Step 5e. Build a Feedback Mechanism for Vendors

It's relatively inevitable that a discrepancy will be discovered between what is mentioned in the questionnaire and the actual practice of the third party. Organizations need a way to address these in constructive, legally informed ways. In the true sense of partnership, establishing a bilateral way to communicate discrepancies or issues is crucial to maintaining the relationship and mitigating risk.

For example, some TPRM vendors may actually *invite* risk into the organization through associated and unintentional practices—making it easier for attackers to gain the critical information they need to compromise the supply chain that affects systems. The irony is that TPRM requires a repository of information to accurately run analytics on, and diagnose any inherent risk from, the third party. However, these repositories and the processes around their use are not always configured or protected in ways that optimally reduce risk to the enterprise (e.g., insecure applications, insecure file transfer). The key is to have a way to assess third parties that allows for a check, or a feedback, on how the third party is actually performing.

The unfortunate reality is that TPRM data is not always protected, not even by the third party tasked to collect such data. Security researchers have indicated there are a noteworthy number of vendors providing third-party risk management services that create an avenue for third-party attacks. A strong TPRM program considers vulnerabilities in cybersecurity risk reduction operations and builds a feedback mechanism for legal and management to communicate with third parties. Also, internally, a thorough review of vendors that have access to critical assets on a regular basis helps identify where vendors may be introducing risk to the organization.

With a feedback mechanism in place and managed properly, it is time to provide some extra safeguards to continue to validate the organization's third-party risk program. To begin aligning third-party risk to contracts, take the following step.

Step 5f. Align to Procurement and Purchasing

Invite the contracts department into the problem. Having language within your contracts that your third parties agree upon is important. It validates the work your third-party risk program has done, and it ensures that the third party is responsible for adhering to your program rules.

TPRM has a key hook into the actual contract established or executed by the primary organization and the third party. Several areas are worth considering. These include the following:

- **Aligning access to critical systems and assets**: Does this vendor have access to critical data, and if so, what safeguards are in place to monitor access?

- **Proper contracts for various vendors**: Are there different contracts for different types of vendors? This is especially important for industrial controls, where some vendors require direct access to operational technology, but not necessarily information technology. Proper contracts for on-premise IT are likely different than those for off-premise, cloud providers, where access is monitored differently.

- **Verifying vendors annually**: Are there contract provisions for verifying vendor-provided security data? Are the contracts reviewed at a frequency (e.g., annually, semiannually) relevant to the assets that the third party accesses?

- **Pulling in training**: Are third parties part of the organizational training or phishing email campaign? How do you verify that third-party individuals know and understand the risks associated with connecting to your assets?

Keep in Mind: Third-Party Risk Management

Many organizations have a sufficient vendor checklist to derive a risk score. Typically, the objective is to prioritize response and assessment. Some organizations look to outside vendors for these scores. Either way, some of these considerations should be kept in mind:

- **Ask the right questions.**

  - **Identify**: What systems or data do they have access to? And what privileged access do they have?

  - **Protect**: How secure are the access points?

  - **Detect**: Do they monitor what is critical?

  - **Respond**: Are they prepared to respond?

  - **Recover**: Are they able to recover properly?

- **Verify the third party knows what data is critical to your organization.**

  - How do they protect that data?

  - How do they assess themselves for vulnerabilities?

  - How are they ready to respond?

- **Align to procurement and purchasing (in contracts).**

  - Which vendors are allowed without a TPRM checklist?

  - Is the right to inspect allowed at any time?

- **Trust but verify.**

  - Check on the TPRM program over time.

Overall, TPRM has become a significant area of focus, as attackers use a *relationship chain* to find ways into organizations. This is not new, but it is challenging. Internal alignment is critical in this area, as buy-in from internal teams (e.g., contracts, legal) is critical in understanding and mitigating the risk. Key internal functions play major roles as GRC, risk, cyber, procurement, and legal all come together to solve this particular risk problem. If there is one major point to remember, the trust but verify[28] proverb might be that point.

Step 6. Pick the Right Tools and Avoid Distraction

Tools! Everyone loves good, automated solutions to solve all of our problems, except, of course, when they don't solve all our problems.

After laying out the current program and associated activities, program gaps have likely emerged. You might notice that some of the gaps can be filled with automated tooling, some with data collection and management solutions, and others with training and education. Either way, defensive services and tools are available to help fill the program gaps and help solve critical needs for the organizational defenses. But first, let's settle on what *tools* mean.

From this point on, tools are considered products and services that provide or enhance the organization's security posture. These fall into categories that align with critical asset classes: data protection (e.g., encryption), device security (e.g., PKI services), application security (e.g., vulnerability scanners), networks (e.g., network defense software, network defense hardware), and users (e.g., training, education). Many

---

[28] Thank you, President Ronald Regan, for bringing this Russian proverb to the American public during the early 1980s nuclear disarmament and nonproliferation.

cybersecurity tools exist, and many claim to solve the most crucial security problem you have. The challenge, however, is picking the right tool for the right problem. Sounds familiar?

Selection begins with solution prioritization. Of the gaps discovered in the program, what is the top priority to solve, and by when does it need a solution? The program worksheet can help. Figure 5-14 illustrates a simple way to capture activity prioritization within the full context of the security program.

FUNCTION	DESCRIPTION	PROPOSED ACTIVITIES	RESPONSIBILITY	DUE DATE	PRIORITY
IDENTIFY	Know the most critical assets	• <Proposed activity> • <Proposed activity> • <Proposed activity>	• <Title, Name> • <Title, Name> • <Title, Name>	• <Date> • <Date> • <Date>	• <Priority> • <Priority> • <Priority>
PROTECT	Establish meaningful safeguards and behaviors around most critical information	• <Proposed activity> • <Proposed activity> • <Proposed activity>	• <Title, Name> • <Title, Name> • <Title, Name>	• <Date> • <Date> • <Date>	• <Priority> • <Priority> • <Priority>
DETECT	Monitor for and discover potential cybersecurity events	• <Proposed activity> • <Proposed activity> • <Proposed activity>	• <Title, Name> • <Title, Name> • <Title, Name>	• <Date> • <Date> • <Date>	• <Priority> • <Priority> • <Priority>
RESPOND	Prepare for and mitigate cybersecurity events	• <Proposed activity> • <Proposed activity> • <Proposed activity>	• <Title, Name> • <Title, Name> • <Title, Name>	• <Date> • <Date> • <Date>	• <Priority> • <Priority> • <Priority>
RECOVER	Reduce the impact and maximize recovery time	• <Proposed activity> • <Proposed activity> • <Proposed activity>	• <Title, Name> • <Title, Name> • <Title, Name>	• <Date> • <Date> • <Date>	• <Priority> • <Priority> • <Priority>

Figure 5-14. *Program worksheet with activity prioritization*

Here, the activities are prioritized against one another to bring shape to the program. The rubric for prioritization should be based on the relative risk profile and acceptance of the organization. Exactly how to prioritize activities is a matter for both management and executives, based on understanding the risk and risk tolerance. But a few resources are available to help with this process.

First, refer back to the risk register. Critical assets and the associated risks should be the starting point. This means the threat landscape, possible vulnerabilities, and anticipated impact to the organization are considered. This exercise also helps ensure proper assessments and assumptions were considered when identifying critical assets and impact categories.

Second, socialize with the security review team (there should be one). Prioritization is nearly impossible with large committees, but inviting the security team into the prioritization focus helps ensure everyone is on the same page for what to do next (someone should be looking for the items not on the list, but that is the nature of security). Defending the choices is just as important as choosing them.

Last, prioritize the activities based on risk, and the program now has a focused set of activities sequenced along relative importance. (Add a timeline to expected activity completion, and it magically becomes a simplified road map.)

Now that prioritization of activities is established, attention can turn back to the gaps and the problem of finding the right tools to fill the gaps. But how? How to best identify the right tool for the right problem? The next step is navigating through the vendor landscape to find the right fit. But this navigation can be distracting in many ways. Fortunately, patterns tend to emerge in each problem where a particular tool may help. The demand for security capabilities automation is real, and the key to resolving this is to ensure the tool solves the right problem.

One possible way to address this is to follow Sounil Yu's Cyber Defense Matrix (CDM).[29] The Cyber Defense Matrix provides a structured and methodical approach to navigating the security vendor marketplace. Using the CDM, you can quickly discern what products solve what problems and be informed on the core function of a given product. For example, the CDM can be used to look across the whole organizational security stack for a complete understanding of what is needed. Figure 5-15 illustrates a version of the CDM.

---

[29] The Cyber Defense Matrix helps map vendor capabilities to functions and assets. Information on it exists at `https://cyberdefensematrix.com`.

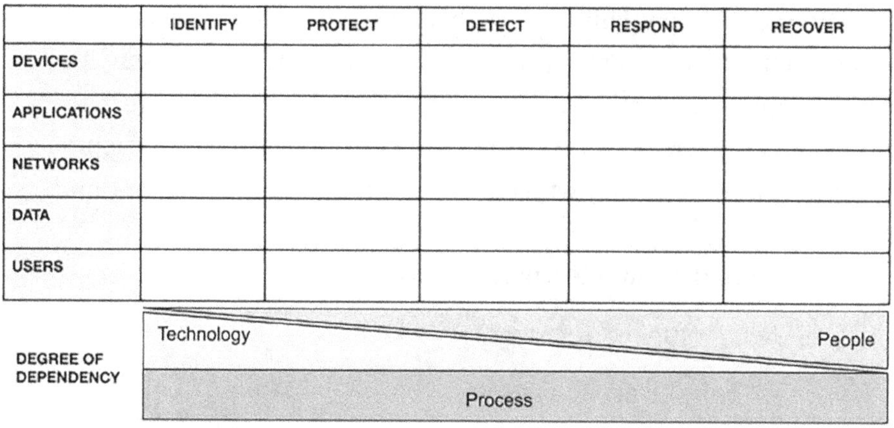

	IDENTIFY	PROTECT	DETECT	RESPOND	RECOVER
DEVICES					
APPLICATIONS					
NETWORKS					
DATA					
USERS					

DEGREE OF DEPENDENCY

Technology ————————————————————————— People

Process

Figure 5-15. *One version of the Cyber Defense Matrix*

The first dimension captures the five operational functions of the NIST CSF. Mapping to management practices is relatively straightforward. Running through the matrix provides a point of view. How secure is the organization? How secure should the organization be? How can the organization get from here to there through what's available in the security marketplace?

Sometimes a significant distraction, finding tools to fill security gaps or enhance capabilities, is not easy. Developing a risk-based prioritization first and then using a framework like the CDM can help resolve the challenge and ensure the right tool solves the right problem.

Set a Program Review Frequency

With a well-defined structured view of organizational cybersecurity risks, managing the risks as a program becomes possible. As the structure allows for planned activities, managers have a focal point to mitigate risks and track progress. However, at this point, the program structure is static—simply a documented set of foundational categories, with activities to address risks and due dates. The program needs action to become a bona fide action plan. This starts with a frequent review—a planned review of current progress toward the assigned due dates. This may seem like a clear and quite obvious point, but taking determined action to review the program is one that many organizations skip. Be sure to set a reasonable program review frequency with the management team, engineers, and executives.

To get started, a few areas may be covered:

- Review the risk register.

  - Is it still accurate?

  - Have the threats changed?

  - Have new vulnerabilities been introduced into the organization?

- Review the activity prioritization.

  - Are the priorities still accurate?

  - Is there one area over-prioritized? (Check for under-prioritized areas such as Respond and Recover.)

- Gain buy-in for the program's next steps.

  - Is the majority of the team on board with the plan?

  - Are the executive or board-level questions answered?

Setting a cybersecurity posture review is essential to maintaining proper cybersecurity management. With due dates assigned to activities, overall categories may be assigned review dates. With a demonstrated coverage of the topics, reviews may mature over time, for example, a full review of where the organization stands on identifying critical assets or the entire Identify function if using the CSF. Revisitation of the current organizational posture helps management maintain active participation in the reduction of cybersecurity risks.

Prepare to Respond and Recover

One major pitfall to avoid is over-indexing on one or two areas when managing a cybersecurity risk program. Many organizations begin and stay dedicated to managing activities that fall under Protect and Detect in the CSF. Naturally, these are the fun and challenging areas of cybersecurity. However, Respond and Recover are the two key areas that focus attention on mitigating the cybersecurity risk *once the risk has become real.*

As an organization focused on reducing the impact of a cybersecurity event, be sure to spend time ensuring that the organization (as a whole) is ready to respond and recover in the event of a true cybersecurity incident.

Two key considerations include as follows:

- Ensure the organization is prepared for and is ready to mitigate a cybersecurity event. This includes ensuring that response plans are up to date and practiced over time.

- Ensure that the organization is ready to recover should something catastrophic happen (e.g., full shutdown due to ransomware). This includes ensuring that business continuity plans are up to date and that procedures are in place and practiced and establishing and practicing failovers for resiliency systems or backup system restoration.

Managing the Problem, a Recap

Overall, simplifying how cybersecurity risk is managed is no easy task in any organization. But a few tools are available to help in the absence of a full cybersecurity program: apply a framework, structure the organization, and prepare to respond and possibly recover.

Plenty of cybersecurity frameworks exist, and no one framework applies perfectly to any one organization. However, an established framework provides a single integrated approach to addressing the cybersecurity risk problem. Employing one helps shape the organizational thinking and the overall enterprise technique around common areas of cybersecurity risks. That structure is the indispensable component of a defendable cybersecurity risk program. Applying a known cybersecurity framework—especially in the absence of one—immediately brings shape to a security practice around common objective-based disciplines in any organization, regardless of industry.

Applying a framework is a fundamental first step in organizing the cybersecurity practice for the enterprise as it sets one approach that fits the business. The key to resolving this is clear management to assign roles (e.g., an adversary, a manager, a third party). Remember, there is a person at the center of the problem you are trying to solve, and the key driver to any problem is a person (e.g., an adversary, a manager, a third party). That is, there is a person at the center of the problem you are trying to manage.

Recent Examples

Example 1. Addressing Too Many Frameworks

Let's continue to follow the organization in Example 1 of Chapter 4. After level-setting on risk and clarifying the assets most valued by the organization, the CISO and team were ready to start assigning cybersecurity initiatives or activities to protect critical assets. Recall the checklist illustrated in Figure 5-16.

☑	Define how we think of cybersecurity risk	Are we all using the same definition of cybersecurity risk across the enterprise?
☑	Know our critical assets	Are our critical assets understood within the enterprise?
☐	Establish clear cybersecurity activities	Are there appropriate cybersecurity activities in place, with people assigned, to address the risk?
☐	Set appropriate measures	Are key areas of cybersecurity risk being measured for risk decision-support?
☐	Prepare to respond	Are we, as an organization, ready to respond in the event of a "cyber" incident?
☐	Know the laws for the industry	Had legal counsel advised on the most current and appropriate care for the information we hold?

Figure 5-16. *Checklist marking the risk understanding portions completed*

The main challenge was that the activities needed a logical structure. Choosing the proper activities based solely on the critical asset process seemed to be a good start but also missing a more holistic view. The CISO and team needed a structure. They asked stakeholders to be included in the next steps of assigning cyber program activities that would extend past the security team.

It turns out each person asked had a different framework they knew and sometimes would reference. Now, the organization had too many frameworks and needed to settle on one. To get here, the team took a combined approach to the steps outlined earlier. They started by inviting individuals with equity into the process. This included contracts, the legal team (for risk understanding), IT, and division managers. They debated what worked well in the industry. The main objective was to balance reporting to regulators, communicate throughout the organization, and align what the board needed to hear. The main frameworks from the teams working the process were the CSF, MITRE ATT&CK, and FAIR. Naturally, there was a bit of a pointed discussion around each of them.

The real defenders in cybersecurity were adamant about the ATT&CK framework. The IT team was passionate about the NIST SP 800-53 for certain controls and understandable ways to address the CIA triad. The legal team was familiar with the FAIR risk model, as they largely heard about its use in defining relevant levels of risk. In a previous discussion with the CISO, they had struggled with the dollar amount calculation and decided to address the risk level first to tell the real risk story.

Over a debate on risk, they settled on one: the CSF, as it acted as a Rosetta stone to communicate the program inside and outside the organization. After one week of discussions and problem-solving meetings, they developed the fundamentals for the cybersecurity program. Figure 5-17 illustrates where they landed.

FUNCTION	DESCRIPTION	CATEGORIES	ACTIVITY	RESPONSIBILITY	DUE DATE
IDENTIFY	Know the most critical assets	• Asset Management • Business Environment • Governance • Risk Assessment/ Strategy • Supply Chain Risk Mgmt	• Complete asset inventory • Critical services under mgmt. • Full cyber risk process in place • Approved risk tolerance • Third-party risk plan in place	• Dir of IT • Dir of IT • CISO • CISO • CRO/Legal	• Q3 (this year) • Q1 (next year) • Q3 (this year) • Q3 (this year) • Q4 (this year)
PROTECT	Establish meaningful safeguards and behaviors around most critical information	• Access Control • Awareness and Training • Data Security • Information Protection • Maintenance • Protective Technology	• User access mgmt. in place • Implement security campaign • Static analysis in place • Secure SDLC in place • No remote maintenance • Removable media denied	• PAM Mgr • Dir of HR • Services Mgr • Services Mgr • Network Mgr • Dir of IT	• Q4 (this year) • Q3 (this year) • Q3 (this year) • Q4 (this year) • Q4 (this year) • Q3 (this year)
DETECT	Monitor for and discover potential cybersecurity events	• Anomalies and Events • Continuous Monitoring • Detection Processes (1) • Detection Processes (2)	• User behavior analysis • Weekly log analysis inspected • Threat feeds integrated • Network detection tool in place	• IR Mgr • IR Mgr • IR Mgr • IR Mgr	• Q4 (this year) • Q4 (this year) • Q1 (next year) • Q1 (next year)
RESPOND	Prepare for and mitigate events	• Response Planning • Communications (internal and external) • Analysis • Mitigation • Improvements (response)	• Response plan developed • Response plan tested • TBD • TBD • TBD	• IR Mgr • IR Mgr • TBD • TBD • TBD	• Q3 (this year) • Q3 (this year) + Q1 (next year) • TBD (w/i 1yr) • TBD (w/i 1yr) • TBD (w/i 2yrs)
RECOVER	Reduce the impact and maximize recovery time	• Recovery planning • Improvements (recovery) • Communications (internal and external)	• Business Continuity plan in place • TBD • TBD	• COO • TBD • TBD	• Q4 (this year) • TBD (w/i 2yrs) • TBD (w/i 2yrs)

Figure 5-17. *Example 1's approach to establishing a practical cybersecurity program*

The cybersecurity defenders discovered the attack mapping to the CSF and worked with the CISO to build an in-depth defense plan across areas where threats could be high. This helped plan out the activities for the next few years. The IT team used the CSF to NIST SP 800-53 mapping, with a few gaps, and level-set on using the CSF to align the IT functions with the CISO security activities. This became a real success story in the organization. The legal team settled on the benefits of level-setting on risk instead of a straight dollar amount. They settled on "% of people covered by PAM" to speak to the real risk level story and address the actual dollar amount later. In the meantime, they reviewed the impact categories as defined in the NISTIR 7621 Revision 1 "Small Business Information Security: The Fundamentals" to get a jump on anticipating costs.

As a bonus, many board members were familiar with the CSF, making recommendations easier since they were speaking to an existing level of understanding.

A clear understanding of accountability and programmatic due dates was established when they assigned initiatives, dates, and roles. This forced a prioritization based on available resources, such as funding, people, and time; items that could not be addressed, based on limited resources, became activities with pushed-out due dates once the resources were available (see italicized parts in Figure 5-17).

Once all the programs were laid out, this immediately identified gaps in programs. Put activities in place for future dates, and set in motion a three-year road map of initiatives (a.k.a. activities), prioritized by risk and resources to address the risk.

At this point, the CISO and team were ready to move forward with measures, as illustrated in Figure 5-18.

☑	Define how we think of cybersecurity risk	Are we all using the same definition of cybersecurity risk across the enterprise?
☑	Know our critical assets	Are our critical assets understood within the enterprise?
☑	Establish clear cybersecurity activities	Are there appropriate cybersecurity activities in place, with people assigned, to address the risk?
☐	Set appropriate measures	Are key areas of cybersecurity risk being measured for risk decision-support?
☐	Prepare to respond	Are we, as an organization, ready to respond in the event of a "cyber" incident?
☐	Know the laws for the industry	Had legal counsel advised on the most current and appropriate care for the information we hold?

Figure 5-18. *Checklist marking the risk understanding and managing portions completed*

Example 2. Many TPRM Tools

A retirement advisory company had multiple tools, methods, and goals for a TPRM initiative that included multiple teams. Information from this developing and dispersed approach was unintelligible, providing more confusion than actionable risk information about third parties. The organization needed one cohesive approach.

To get started, the organization started at the strategic level. They created a corporate third-party risk management initiative. This initiative had one strategic objective: zero information security breaches due to a third party.

With alignment from the top, a team was dedicated to the initiative, charged with ultimately identifying what risk third parties were introducing into the organizational landscape and then identifying ways to reduce that risk to achieve the strategic objective.

This team formed a cross-practice group to address the risk and get buy-in. The cross-practice group included one person from each group: risk management, cybersecurity, purchasing, and legal. With alignment to the strategic objective, meetings and tasks were set up for engaging, efficient, and effective decisions. This group even included an internal feedback mechanism of ten third-party vendors in compliance per week to keep them on track.

The cross-practice group first developed a sufficient vendor questionnaire checklist to provide a prioritized response and assessment. This checklist started with the basic questions needing to be satisfied for each function aligned to their framework of choice: the CSF. Figure 5-19 lays out the high-level questions.

FUNCTION	DESCRIPTION	QUESTION (High Level)
IDENTIFY	Know the most critical information.	What systems or data do they have access to?
PROTECT	Establish meaningful safeguards and behaviors around the most critical information.	What privileged access do they have?
DETECT	Monitor for and discover potential cybersecurity events.	Can they detect anomalous activity?
RESPOND	Prepare for and mitigate cybersecurity events.	Are they prepared to respond?
RECOVER	Reduce the impact and maximize recovery time.	Do they have business continuity and disaster recovery measures in place, if all else fails?

Figure 5-19. *High-level questions used to get started on a TPRM questionnaire*

Aligning to these questions set the team to begin asking vendors the right questions. For example, they began to focus on an organization's ability to answer the following:

- Do you know what data is critical to your organization?

- How do you protect that data?

- How do you assess yourself for vulnerabilities?

- Are you ready to respond?

The purchasing agreements and contracts were updated to act as a control or forcing mechanism. Included in contractual language and policies were controls such as the following:

- No fully executed vendor agreement without a TPM questionnaire.

- The organization maintains the right to inspect vendors to verify questions at any time.

With these items in place, the group settled on establishing a review process for every quarter. Each quarter, the program was reviewed to refine questions, eliminate overly burdensome questions, and check in on the overall objective: zero information security breaches due to a third party.

Overall, the organization was able to get started on a basic TPM program. A few lessons were learned for improvement that went beyond the scope of just getting started during the process:

- **Tactical matters**: The actual individuals connecting to systems are a key risk. Ranking third-party organizations matters, but it's the individual who introduces risk to company systems. Developing a way to hold the actual individual accountable helps create incentives to reach the goal of zero information security breaches.

- **Feedback loops**: Building in a feedback loop, once the program is in place, helps provide critical data to inform how the project is going. The questionnaire helps get started, and "trust but verify" helps keep it going. Two key feedback mechanisms can inform progress toward a goal of zero information security breaches: (1) asset management, which is percentage of data classified as critical/non-critical, and (2) governance, which percentage of cybersecurity policies established and communicated.

- **Spot-checking vendors**: Not all vendors perform consistently with answers on the questionnaires. Performing a "spot check" or a quick assessment of key areas once per year helps verify the vendors are keeping with the answers on the questionnaire.

Example 3. From Controls Focus to a Risk Strategy

A large insurance company had recently merged with an existing healthcare organization. Both organizations had a pre-existing cybersecurity program to meet their respected regulations and standards. Both were directed to combine programs under one CISO—providing a centralized cyber service for the newly merged entity. Both programs had different sets of policies and controls to comply with the multiple compliance and regulatory needs of each business. Neither organization, however, had a streamlined way of addressing the risk to the organization or an informed way to view tolerance needed to move past compliance. Lacking this strong orientation to risk, they needed a top-down strategic approach to align both programs without disrupting the current status or sacrificing control accuracy.

The approach they took was a blend of strategic and tactical. On the strategic side, they decided to choose one framework, the NIST CSF, to bring together the multiple security, privacy, and other regulatory requirements like ISO/IEC 27001, Payment Card Industry Data Security Standard (PCI DSS), and NIST SP 800-53r3 controls. The overall goal was to get to a point where the single CISO role could view the top ten risks in cybersecurity faced by the newly formed organization.

The CSF-provided mapping to NIST 800-53r3 was used to align controls, and the HITRUST common security framework[30] was used for mapping the new approach to the ISO/IEC 27001 and PCI DSS controls already in use.

With this in place, they tackled the hardest job next: identifying the newly combined critical assets. Fortunately, one of the organizations had begun creating a robust asset management system. The existence of this process helped get started on tackling the newly formed organization. This effort took a significant amount of time but provided a view into the risks that allowed the organization to accurately report the top ten risks.

On the tactical side, the organization aligned existing processes and tools to this newly formed view of risk. With a pre-existing security operations center (SOC) and some pre-existing tooling, they moved forward with a way to identify the sources of risk information necessary to feed this top ten process. This included areas to help address the risks:

- **Incidents**: The ability to track items to be investigated by someone in the SOC. To do this, they implemented *security information and event management* (SIEM) with a vendor. Discovering the need to automate routine activities, they brought in *security, orchestration, automation, and response* (SOAR) tools, providing analysts a way to guide actions when similar incidents arise; this informed a set of predefined playbooks of automated steps.

---

[30] The Health Information Trust Alliance (HITRUST) offers a common security framework. HITRUST is an organization governed by representatives from the healthcare industry.

- **Remediation:** They developed an incident response playbook for specific roles (e.g., HR, legal, executive) to ensure the organization could respond to an incident, thereby reducing risk as it happens. Anticipating these results, the organization planned two new activities for a later date: one separate subsystem that handled all plans for all risks and a person responsible for monitoring, managing, and remediation.

With this in place, the organization set a risk target based on the top ten. It began choosing appropriate measures for measuring risk reduction along the lines of an inherent exposure risk rating, which allowed for various application risk ratings to fit into an overall operational risk assessment to include residual risk aligned to the CSF.

The following are lessons learned along the way:

- **Start at the top.** Taking an approach of the risks from the top down provided a centralized view needed to line up standards and controls and inform the top ten risks in the organization. This helped focus efforts on the risks on which the standards and controls were based.

- **Have a playbook.** During the alignment to risk, a drawback from the SOAR implementations was discovered: the lack of an action playbook. While the SOAR helped with the context enrichment of the alerts, the newly formed organization needed a fundamental understanding of how their processes reduced risk. They developed a playbook to run certain alerts through many what-if situations, providing a better understanding of the risks.

Example 4. Third-Party Without a Checklist

When third-party risk management was still the major problem to be focused on, circa 2017, a consulting firm decided it was time to begin creating and managing their own third parties before it came back to haunt them.

At the time, however (and still to this day), the firm and organizations struggled with defining where their third-party risk assessments would live and who would manage the third parties throughout their life cycle. Furthermore, and maybe most importantly, they struggled to figure out how to judge the risk the third party presented to their organization.

This consulting firm started with the tools-first approach. Although "tools-first" is not always the best strategy, this organization went in with a plan and a very strategic reason for the "tools-first" approach.

The firm picked a vendor tool to create a vendor/third-party checklist to automatically assess the third party's potential risk to their firm. How did they do this? This firm was focused on automation and efficiency. While they would have third-party risk assessors checking up on the third parties throughout their life cycle, they wanted their questionnaire process to be seamless. So they followed a simple 1-2-3 approach.

First, they created questions for each category of their questionnaire. This organization, like many others, decided on the framework and the risks they were most worried about (i.e., what were the biggest risks to their organization). For example, this consulting firm chose categories like *reputational risk* and *operational risk*. Once the framework and the biggest risks were decided upon, the team worked with the vendor to design the questionnaire as input to the tool.

Second, as the team created the questionnaire, they would rank each question with a specific score. This questionnaire included a drop-down list of potential answers the vendor could choose from. Depending upon the answers the vendor came up with, nested questions would appear. Most of the time, nested questions only appeared if the vendor answered in a way that posed more risk rather than less. The nested questions were normally free text fields that required a third-party assessor to manually go in and verify or follow up with the vendor.

Third and last, at the end of the questionnaire, the vendor would fall into critical, high, medium, or low risk based on how they filled in the questionnaire. If a vendor was at a critical or high, they were reassessed with more frequency (i.e., quarterly) than the medium- and low-risk vendors (i.e., yearly), and specific contract language was added to manage the risk. There was also the potential that if the organization decided that the vendor was not worth the risk, business would not commence. This meant the risk the vendor could potentially add was too much for the consulting firm's diet with their risk exposure. Essentially the question they were asking themselves was if this risk was too much.

While this seems as though this was a flawless implementation of a third-party risk management tool and checklist, there were plenty of roadblocks as the organization went. Remember the high-level question used to get started on a TPRM questionnaire? (See Figure 5-20.) Well, believe it or not, the organization struggled the most with finding the right questions to ask to receive the most accurate picture of the vendor. The tool automation relied heavily on the correct weight being added to the risk-based questions.

FUNCTION	DESCRIPTION	QUESTION (High Level)
IDENTIFY	Know the most critical information.	What systems or data do they have access to?
PROTECT	Establish meaningful safeguards and behaviors around the most critical information.	What privileged access do they have?
DETECT	Monitor for and discover potential cybersecurity events.	Can they detect anomalous activity?
RESPOND	Prepare for and mitigate cybersecurity events.	Are they prepared to respond?
RECOVER	Reduce the impact and maximize recovery time.	Do they have business continuity and disaster recovery measures in place, if all else fails?

Figure 5-20. *High-level questions used to get started on a TPRM questionnaire*

Although it took more time to put together a firm questionnaire than anticipated, the organization was glad they spent the extra time weighing and asking the right questions. It helped them in the future when assessing, determining, and maturing their potential third-party risk scores.

Throughout this process, the team learned a few key lessons:

- **Content is most important**. While the tools-first approach worked, the consulting firm realized the actual content of the questionnaire would give them the biggest return as opposed to the automation built into the tool.

- **Strategy is key**. The tool's first tactic was successful mainly due to the strategic planning and effort before beginning the journey with the vendor. Always plan, and avoid scrambling and crisis decision-making as much as possible.

- **Be proactive rather than reactive**. While this firm was lucky to get ahead of the curve or right along the curve of third-party risk management, they watched some of their peers fall victim to third-party incidents and scramble. Prioritize security when you can.

Pitfalls to Avoid

Managing cybersecurity risk has its challenges. Avoiding several pitfalls at the onset of a cybersecurity program can help move the organization toward insightful risk management.

The following are common pitfalls to avoid:

- **Pitfall 1**: Finding the "perfect" framework. Searching for the one framework that fits the organization perfectly can slow down progress. No single framework fits any organization's risk profile perfectly. Starting with a published framework to guide the program provides a structure, or at least a starting point, to align cybersecurity activities and outcomes to business objectives.

- **Pitfall 2**: Using a custom framework that does not map to regulators or industry. Staying up to speed with the applicable laws and regulations is hard enough. Choosing a framework that does not map nicely to regulatory requirements can simply add intense analytic gymnastics when demonstrating security and compliance to outside parties.

- **Pitfall 3**: Failing to assign one lead with specific deadlines and appropriate resources. When it comes to cybersecurity, who has the lead for certain projects and activities needs to be clear. Risk mitigation efforts need guidance and ownership. Absent clear responsibilities, risks tend to get worse.

CHAPTER 6

Get Ready for Measures

Introduction

Articulating the risk and establishing a program is a mammoth task in effectively managing the risk to the business. The final step is determining the measurements that will provide the most value while avoiding "distraction" measures.

Overall, a proper cybersecurity management program contains output values in key areas used for decision support. A proper program runs like a decision support system, providing an appropriate measurement of the problem being managed—in this case, cybersecurity risk.

Strategically placed measures within the program, assigned to key cyber risk areas, support tactical and strategic decisions on where to apply resources to address the risk that may impact a critical operational need of the organization. In some cases, values from cyber risk measures act as a specific gauge for progress toward achieving a specified risk-acceptable goal, for example, reducing the number of out-of-date operating systems to zero across the entire organization. In other cases, values from cyber risk measures act as a conjecture about possible risk-inducing activities that require investigation, for example, the number of employees demonstrating poor security behavior. In all cases, values from cybersecurity program measures need to provide insights to solve the overall risk problem. Every organization manages cyber risk differently. Whichever program management method is chosen, identifying the key areas for program-related improvement is critical for decision-making, but this is not so simple.

Organizations face two common problems when embarking on measures for cybersecurity risk reduction: (1) failure to take a broad view of the risk and (2) the inability to collect proper data from within the organization. Before jumping into the development of specific measures for the first time, it is helpful to ensure that these two areas are sufficiently addressed.

To get started, take a broad view of cybersecurity risk within the organization. This means thinking through and anticipating the impact based on the categories addressed and the key areas of business operations that need to be monitored; these are the areas that help provide meaningful signals of increased risk or, conversely, reduced risk. Typically, a broad view centers around three areas: (1) threats to, or possible malicious actions against, the organization; (2) access to, or use of, critical assets; and (3) ability to mitigate an action, once discovered. Narrowly defining the overall risk creates blind spots in organizational risk monitoring; for example, simply focusing on protecting critical assets leaves the organization blind to the ability to respond to the inevitable incident.

Next, let's think about some of the measures themselves. Program performance and objective-tracking measures will come into play later, but overall risk indicators are the focus for now.

There are a few concepts to keep in mind.

Keep in Mind: Consider the Broad View of Risk for Measurement

Many organizations struggle to get started with appropriate cybersecurity risk measures. Typically, the objective is to provide feedback on risk reduction; however, many measures slide into program progress. Keep in mind that cybersecurity risk measures should be

- Actionable

- Addressable

- Insightful

With these considerations in mind, begin to formulate a few key risk measures that signal risk. Recall that measures begin at the top, strategic areas of risk. Brainstorming the key areas of organizational risk can help broaden the scope. What is most important to the organization as a whole? What are we not thinking about?

There are two pitfalls to avoid when thinking about measures. The first is the *easy approach* of developing less-than-informative measures that can be measured immediately at the peril of a longer-term informative, actionable, insightful measure. The second is the *immediate solution approach* of developing measures from one or two ideas to provide immediate solutions at the peril of continuing to think through options for truly insightful risks. When working on ways to measure cybersecurity risk, the aspiration should be to provide, at the strategic level, values that support organizational risk reduction decisions and efforts. Should this be accomplished, look deep into the organization for authoritative data sources to feed the measures.

Management teams often struggle with both the actual math and the authoritative data sources to formulate a measure that provides an insightful value. Chances are that the data needed to feed the measure will

143

not be readily available. Some find this a sticking point. However, a lack of data does not mean the measure is wrong; it just means the value cannot be calculated or derived immediately. When faced with the absence of either a clear equation or a required data source, avoid the tendency to drop the measure altogether for something easier. Instead, develop an interim measure to act as a surrogate to the harder measure until the data, or the equation, is available; just because the data simply cannot be pulled from current sources is no reason to abandon a proper measure.

Once measures are determined, data sources may be identified or constructed to derive the proper value. This is where the maturity journey begins—the quest to achieve meaningful results from data and sources at all levels of the organization. But the maturity journey is not one-directional downward; it is also upward and outward, as the understanding of the risk begins to drive more insightful and meaningful strategic indicators of risk. After a few risk-reporting cycles, real risk-insightful data is often discovered within an organization—typically by security engineers at the front lines of the security efforts. Security engineers typically have the best view of where the tactical risks live. The management challenge is to balance the overall number of measures with the vast amount of data engineers can provide on a day-to-day basis. Here, the overall cybersecurity program or strategy comes into play since the proper measures are reviewed regularly. The ability to respond to the value provided by these measures also comes into play.

With this context in mind, the act of measuring the problem begins. Picking up from Chapter 5's framework and applied structure with assigned activities, it's time to think about the best data to provide proper risk reduction signals on how well the program addresses identified risks.[1]

---

[1] Note that risk reduction is the objective to be measured. Program performance and individual reactions are currently absent.

CHAPTER 7

Measure the Problem

Introduction

There is an art to metrics. Which measures quantify uncertainty in a way that provides decision-makers with the right mix of risk mitigation and coverage? The ones that serve the overall understanding of a healthy, efficient, and organizationally focused program. Sounds simple? It's not.

Let's face it: metrics are hard. Executive boards are requesting *risk reduction measures* in support of overall organizational objectives. Anticipating and accurately identifying what to measure and report at the executive level requires cyber risk reduction insight and data availability integration within areas of uncertainty that represent the overall business.

Operational leaders are requesting *performance-related measures* to gauge performance effectiveness according to a prescribed set of objectives. The ability to identify what to measure and track at the operational level requires the proper scope to measure the appropriate objectives and informative values to ensure that the measures tell the whole story.

Whatever the value of the measure is set to inform, the overall objective is to evaluate and address risk. The primary focus of measuring cybersecurity is to *quantify uncertainty* in a way that provides decision-makers the appropriate level of risk mitigation and coverage through measurement. Performance indicators and other objective-based measures support the overall risk reduction.

© Ryan Leirvik 2023
R. Leirvik, *Understand, Manage, and Measure Cyber Risk*,
https://doi.org/10.1007/978-1-4842-9319-5_7

The main challenge is that few good measures in cybersecurity are innate at the onset of a cybersecurity program. Good measures are cultivated, fostered, or even acquired over time. And truly good measures mature as the organization better understands the real cybersecurity risk posture.

Providing meaningful measures of risk and maturity typically takes time within any organization. Starting out, key measures should speak to actionable risk reduction (e.g., the elapsed time from incident to response team action, the elapsed time from initial exploitation to discovery). In large organizations, good measures speak to the individual business units to get them involved in understanding and addressing the real cybersecurity risks (e.g., percentage of the supply chain under end-to-end control, number of assets identified as critical). And, overall, good measures should align to strategic, board-level measures supported by tactical measures. After all, the main point of measuring risk in cybersecurity is to understand what is at risk and the organizational ability to manage that risk.

Rules to Follow

Some immediate challenges need to be addressed to start measuring organizational cybersecurity risk. The first is agreement among executives and managers on the actual risks to measure. The second is which measures provide an accurate representation of the risks. And the natural follow-on challenge to these two revolves around the actual ability to find and process data available to feed the measure. A sequence of rules exists to help address these challenges, some of which have embedded steps for further guidance.

```
┌─────────────────────────────────────────────────────┐
│           RULES TO FOLLOW: MEASURE THE PROBLEM        │
└─────────────────────────────────────────────────────┘
```

The following are six basic rules in measuring cybersecurity risk.

TAKEAWAYS

- **Rule 1:** Chose informative measures that provide actionable values.

- **Rule 2:** Research what others have done (measures that have worked).

- **Rule 3:** Be clear on the math.

- **Rule 4:** Gain buy-in from stakeholders.

- **Rule 5:** Develop a reporting structure for consistency.

- **Rule 6:** Allow your measures to mature over time.

Choose Informative Measures That Provide Actionable Values

What an organization chooses to measure in cybersecurity indicates the level at which they view the security problem. The objective is to quantify uncertainty in a way that provides decision-makers with the appropriate level of risk mitigation and coverage through measurement. Practically, this means helping to understand the relevant risk in order to adequately protect assets, and the organization, from harm. Choosing insightful measures for managing risk, such as the time from vulnerability discovery to remediation, can indicate a tighter view on risk over simply informational facts, like the number of DDoS attacks over a certain period. And the sheer number of measures an organization uses at the organizational level indicates the maturity of the measures, that is, the ability for the total strategic measures to account for the appropriate measurement of risk. Many organizations keep strategic measures aligned alongside broad functions, like the five CSF functions, with no more than 15 to track key risk areas.

At this point, the risk is understood: protecting critical assets. The action of choosing an appropriate risk-informative set of measures may be broken down into key components for measuring this risk. These components may be the fundamentals for key performance indicators (KPIs), key risk indicators (KRIs), objectives and key results (OKRs), as well as simple measures. These measures may help management through feedback metrics. Figure 7-1 illustrates some of these areas to measure and provides possible measures to apply.

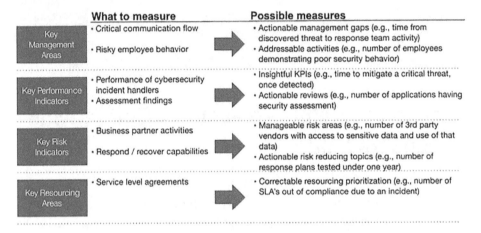

What to measure | **Possible measures**

Key Management Areas
- Critical communication flow
- Risky employee behavior

→
- Actionable management gaps (e.g., time from discovered threat to response team activity)
- Addressable activities (e.g., number of employees demonstrating poor security behavior)

Key Performance Indicators
- Performance of cybersecurity incident handlers
- Assessment findings

→
- Insightful KPIs (e.g., time to mitigate a critical threat, once detected)
- Actionable reviews (e.g., number of applications having security assessment)

Key Risk Indicators
- Business partner activities
- Respond / recover capabilities

→
- Manageable risk areas (e.g., number of 3rd party vendors with access to sensitive data and use of that data)
- Actionable risk reducing topics (e.g., number of response plans tested under one year)

Key Resourcing Areas
- Service level agreements

→
- Correctable resourcing prioritization (e.g., number of SLA's out of compliance due to an incident)

Figure 7-1. *Areas to measure and possible measures to apply*

Before moving into guiding steps for informative measures, there are some helpful points to consider. First, many managers in organizations find themselves digesting a "metric ton" of data. Trying to solve all the available data at once will simply exacerbate the challenge in mind-bending ways. Starting with the problem to solve is a top-down approach. Starting with data available is a bottom-up problem. Approaching the problem from the top down to the bottom helps stay focused on solving the problem: the security of critical assets. To solve it this way, keep in mind the fundamental categories of risk, like the CSF functions (i.e., identifying, protecting, detecting, responding, and recovering), and what goes into the risk categories. This helps keep the attention where it belongs: on the problem being solved.

Second, categorize data into well-defined categories before looking deep into the organization for what data is available. The chosen framework should help guide these categories, such as data loss prevention (Detect) and incident response data (Respond).

With this in mind, it is time to choose measures. Following these steps can help guide the selection of informative measures.

How to Choose Informative Measures

These steps may help you begin choosing informative strategic measures:

- **Step 1.** Choose actionable measures.

- **Step 2.** Define clear addressable activities.

- **Step 3.** Provide actionable reviews.

Step 1. Choose Actionable Measures

"There are three kinds of lies: lies, damned lies, and statistics."[1] When choosing any measure, keep in mind that anything can be measured to prove any point. This notion is precisely the opposite of the objective in cybersecurity. The values of any measure should help support an actionable decision in *managing* the risk around protecting what is critical. The outcome of each measure should be relevant to the discussion of reducing risk.

Actionable measures provide key insights into the level of risk currently associated with what the organization values. These insights support resource decision-making to the risk: time, money, people, and attention. Getting this information accurate is crucial.

---

[1] Who originally said this? Sir Charles Dilke? Do we know it best because of Mark Twain/Samuel Langhorne Clemens? It certainly was not someone in cybersecurity because electronic computer networking did not exist in the 1800s.

To choose actionable measures, first settle on what is valuable to the organization (the *risk register*, informed by asset management). Next, choose up to five categories that strongly represent the risk (refer to the framework chosen); included should be threats, controls, policies, and response at a minimum. Then, determine what mix of risk-, performance-, and objective-based indicators are needed to tell the real risk story.

Some measures may identify management gaps (e.g., time from discovered threat to response team activity). Some provide performance insights (e.g., time to mitigate a critical threat, once detected). And others provide possible indicators of risk (e.g., number of employees demonstrating poor behavior).

Step 2. Define Clear Addressable Activities

With a set of categories chosen for applying measures, choose a set of addressable activities that home in on the due care of critical assets and threats against them. The following are a few examples:

- **Phishing campaigns** as an activity fit under Awareness and Training, paving the way for a key risk indicator of the number of employees demonstrating poor security behavior.[2]

- **Third-party contracts** fit under Access Control, paving the way for a possible key risk indicator of the number of third-party vendors with access to sensitive data and the use of that data.

---

[2]Using only the results from an internal phishing campaign, or set of campaigns, could be considered a narrow view of this measure. Results from the campaign, however, could be considered a starting point, with the intent to mature the measure over time by adding other components of poor behavior; for example, DLP triggers or insider threat triggers.

- **Response plans** fit under Response Planning, paving the way for an actionable risk-reducing measure of the number of response plans tested under one year.

Pulling this all together might look like the table shown in Figure 7-2, which adds a Measure column in place of Priority from the worksheet.

FUNCTION	DESCRIPTION	PROPOSED ACTIVITIES	RESPONSIBILITY	DUE DATE	MEASURE
IDENTIFY	Know the most critical assets	• \<Proposed activity\> • \<Proposed activity\>	• \<Title, Name\> • \<Title, Name\>	• \<Date\> • \<Date\>	• \<KPI/KRI/M\> • \<KPI/KRI/M\>
PROTECT	Establish meaningful safeguards and behaviors around most critical information	• \<Proposed activity\> • \<Proposed activity\> • \<Proposed activity\> • \<Proposed activity\>	• \<Title, Name\> • \<Title, Name\> • \<Title, Name\> • \<Title, Name\>	• \<Date\> • \<Date\> • \<Date\> • \<Date\>	• \<KPI/KRI/M\> • \<KPI/KRI/M\> • \<KPI/KRI/M\> • \<KPI/KRI/M\>
DETECT	Monitor for and discover potential cybersecurity events	• \<Proposed activity\> • \<Proposed activity\> • \<Proposed activity\>	• \<Title, Name\> • \<Title, Name\> • \<Title, Name\>	• \<Date\> • \<Date\> • \<Date\>	• \<KPI/KRI/M\> • \<KPI/KRI/M\> • \<KPI/KRI/M\>
RESPOND	Prepare for and mitigate events	• \<Proposed activity\> • \<Proposed activity\>	• \<Title, Name\> • \<Title, Name\>	• \<Date\> • \<Date\>	• \<KPI/KRI/M\> • \<KPI/KRI/M\>
RECOVER	Reduce the impact and maximize recovery time	• \<Proposed activity\> • \<Proposed activity\>	• \<Title, Name\> • \<Title, Name\>	• \<Date\> • \<Date\>	• \<KPI/KRI/M\> • \<KPI/KRI/M\>

Figure 7-2. *Worksheet for aligning activities to measures, with responsible parties and due dates*

Step 3. Provide Actionable Reviews

Once the activities are set and measures are applied, the challenge of accuracy and relevancy begins. The threat landscape and vulnerable pathways can change by the minute in extreme cases. Program reviews frequently support this while the organization works through the measure maturity process. Establishing and working actionable reviews over time helps ensure the security program has its own security assessment.

Reviewing the program at a specified cadence helps with appropriate resourcing decisions and a feedback mechanism for how well the organization understands the risk. For organizations that are service providers, customer-facing resources may also be impacted. For example, resource prioritization may become critical if a cybersecurity event affects the ability to provide service. Actionable reviews can provide significant insights into anticipating resource balancing and new measures, such as the "number of SLAs out of compliance due to an incident" under the Recovery Planning activity.

Research What Others Have Done (Measures That Have Worked)

Before developing clear measures and supporting math for the organization, check the current status of new and existing measures. At this point, the problem being solved and the objective to be met by measures should be clear. This is a great starting point for research into cybersecurity measures. Why now? A framed perspective of what the organization needs to measure will help categorize measures that fit and measures that do not. The plethora of available ways to measure various risks can be quite daunting when the goal or scope is not clear. Having a strong idea of what is needed before looking to the outside improves the chances that the selected measures are useful to the organization.

Also, keep in mind that cybersecurity is still a maturing field. When it comes to proper measures, plenty of authoritative resources exist to comb for applicable measures. Look to organizations that view the problem from a broad security lens, like organizations that cover multiple industries or cover national-level problems. These organizations may help choose insightful strategic measures. For example, the Cyberspace Solarium Commission recommended establishing a Bureau of Cyber Statistics in the United States.

Research what others have done successfully to see what is new before jumping into the next step for measures.

Measures That Have Worked

As an example of some measures that have worked for other organizations, Figure 7-3 features several program-relevant KPIs, KRIs, and measures aligned to a CSF activity to assign management and accountability to a measure.

FUNCTION	DESCRIPTION	...	MEASURE
IDENTIFY	Know the most critical assets	• ... • ... • ... • ...	• % of assets identified as critical • % of employees passing annual Application Management Policy Awareness training • number of out-of-date systems operating • % of supply chain under end-to-end control
PROTECT	Establish meaningful safeguards and behaviors around most critical information	• ... • ... • ... • ... • ... • ... • ...	• % of privileged accounts are under privileged access control • % of Applications monitored for appropriate data quality use • number of employees demonstrating poor security behavior • Number of applications having security assessment • Mean time to patch (Date from when vuln comes out to when it is ACTUALLY patched) • number of business lines completing business-line application assessments • number of 3rd party vendors with access to sensitive data and use of that data
DETECT	Monitor for and discover potential cybersecurity events	• ...	• time from discovered threat to response team activity
RESPOND	Prepare for and mitigate cybersecurity events	• ...	• time to mitigate a critical threat, once detected
RECOVER	Reduce the impact and maximize recovery time	• ... • ...	• number of response plans tested under one year • number of SLA's out of compliance due to an incident

Figure 7-3. Measures aligned to the CSF

At the program level, measures should be able to tell the risk story for the organization. Typically, this is told through categorical measures that, collectively, add up to the whole story. Deeper, more tactical measures may help inform program measures but should not necessarily provide whole-of-program insights. Arguably, feedback measures for governance and standard setting may elevate to the program level, depending on the nature of the organization and the industry in which the organization operates.

Be Clear About the Math

Mathematics is a very broad and powerful subject. Mathematics made the Internet possible. Mathematics made the computer possible. Mathematics allowed Galileo to challenge man's thinking of Earth's position relative to the sun. Over time, the ability to identify patterns, anticipate next steps, and get ahead of adversaries is a realistic goal for defenders of critical organizational assets in cyber. At this time, however, these are not the intended uses of mathematics for starting a cybersecurity risk management program.[3] With some simple analysis, basic arithmetic is all that is needed to get started in measuring what works at the program level.

The main challenge is not the math. It is the data needed to provide the value. With agreement on what to measure as completed, breaking down the properties to find the data needed to solve the measure becomes the next challenge. It must be done without sacrificing the math or the objective. Two examples help illustrate the key points.

Straight Math

First, let's discuss asset management by looking at "% of assets classified as critical" in Figure 7-3. This measure provides a value useful in helping the organization understand what is at risk. It helps define the organization's view of the core cybersecurity problem: the confidentiality, integrity, and availability of specific assets.

When aligned to an asset management activity (e.g., an asset management system), this measure may be calculated using the straightforward arithmetic shown in Figure 7-4.

---

[3] Arguably, math can solve the entire cybersecurity problem for an organization, providing quite the advantage. An enjoyable and worthwhile discussion, provided an appropriate budget. However, this is a book on the basics of cybersecurity risk program creation. The very basics will be covered here.

Measure	Calculation
% of Assets classified as critical	Number of Critical Assets / Number of Total Assets

Figure 7-4. *Straightforward calculation of an asset management risk measure*

Straight division is all that is needed to calculate the measure. Simple, right? It seems like it. But where does the data come from?

Again, math is not the problem here. The problem is the availability of data to calculate the measure. Does the organization have a full inventory of assets to populate the denominator? Of those assets, is it clear which are critical and which are not?

The total number of assets and the total number of critical assets are needed to complete the calculation. Most, if not all, organizations struggle with this very simple measure. This point illustrates the beauty of simple math applied to a cybersecurity program at the top level. An inability to populate a simple risk measure indicates that the organization does not have a clear view of what is most valuable. Even without the calculated value, the sheer presence of the measure has already begun to accomplish the intent: providing a program-level indication of risk.

What the organization chooses to do next, once exposed to a pure, incalculable measure, begins to define the organization's risk tolerance or acceptable level of risk. The organization can choose to set a lower standard of measure or aim to achieve the hard-to-calculate. Either way, the actions will define it even without authoritatively communicating the risk level (more on this later in the chapter).

Less-Than-Straight Math

Awareness and training might be measured by looking at the "number of employees demonstrating poor security behavior" example from Figure 7-3. A number of variables may feed this measure, depending on the level of information available as well as what insights the measure is intended to provide.

One option is to provide a low, or "beginning," indication of risk. A straight math approach may be used for this option. That includes using the number of employees failing internal phishing campaigns, adding the count that the same employee triggers a data loss protection (DLP) event or violates the acceptable use policy (AUP). This type of measure provides a reasonable starting point for determining possible risky employee behavior.

The other option is to provide a high, or "mature," indication of risk, building off the low indicator by adding expected employee behavior.

Measuring expected employee behavior is a challenge since the measure must map against anomalies. The key is to first identify what the concern is: is it an insider threat or basic poor behavior? Each has "tells" (e.g., performance indicators) and motivators (e.g., financial, malicious) and ultimately boils down to behavior analysis: motive, access, and ability.

One way to calculate this view is to break down metrics relative to the categories:

- **Access**: Identifies who has access to files (the number of accounts under privileged access management (PAM), access to data).

- **Ability**: Identifies who has the technical ability to pull files (e.g., system admin). Were they provided abilities outside the expected role (i.e., not expected to go to system admin)?

- **Motivation**: Identifies financial motivation (e.g., underpaid, in financial distress, philosophical issue).

Indicator data sources may be poor performance data directly from human resources (HR). Ideally, this data would be received *before* the employee has a poor performance review or an AUP violation.

Figure 7-5 features ways both could be calculated based on high- and low-risk indicators.

Measure: Number of employees demonstrating poor security behavior	Calculation
High Indicator	Poor Performance + Access to Controlled Data + Role-based Ability / Total number of Employees
Low Indicator	Number of Employees Failing Phishing + Same Employee Failing DLP or Violating AUP / Total number of Employees

Figure 7-5. *Possible calculation of an employee behavior risk measure*

Whatever math is used, be prepared for two challenges: the ability to determine the data available for measures and the path to measure the interim to the final based on the availability of data. Then, invite others into the problem and socialize the measures.

Gain Buy-In from Stakeholders

A significant program blocker for most leaders in cybersecurity is the ability to communicate the impact of the activities within the cybersecurity program. Leaders are challenged with the need to report both upward and downward and build alliances with other key leaders within the organization for help with activities outside of the classic information security role. For example, third-party risk management requires a working relationship with procurement and legal counsel or contracting to ensure that new purchases or contracted outside parties fall within specific security standards and abide by established controls.

Building key relationships is critical in organization-wide cybersecurity activities as various parts of the organization are essential in achieving successful outcomes of a cybersecurity program. But building these relationships has its challenges, especially when it comes to a difficult-to-understand subject matter, like cybersecurity.

Organizational incentives can help address this problem from the strategic level by providing measures that matter. For example, elements of cybersecurity can be part of executive or management performance (e.g., protection of critical organizational assets, sufficient safeguards against client/customer information, satisfactory training results for management teams). Organizations that take cybersecurity seriously have performance incentives in place that can be measured and reported on over time.

Individual incentives can help in the absence of, or even support, organizational incentives. Let's face it: cybersecurity is not a well-understood discipline within classic management teams. As an incentive, cybersecurity professionals can create a way for others to understand and help manage cybersecurity from their current position.

One way to do this is to invite others into the problem based on their area of expertise. The "number of employees demonstrating poor security behavior" helps inform the cybersecurity program. For example, HR is an employee-facing, service-oriented organizational department that regularly opens a wide variety of document types (e.g., .pdf, .docx, .xlsx, .jpeg). They also have access to critical data (e.g., OSHA records, personally identifiable information, confidentiality agreements, performance appraisals). HR is lush with opportunities for employees to accidentally demonstrate poor security behavior. Working with HR teams to collectively think through the impact of a cybersecurity event may garner support within these teams, as a dual incentive to learn about the dangers of opening attachments and protecting the organization from one of the front lines. If not HR, then perhaps another area within the organization that routinely demonstrates poor security hygiene by employees. Either way, gaining support and buy-in from others can help support the organization's cybersecurity mission. Each person in the organization can help be accountable for reducing the causes or consequences of an incident.

Develop a Reporting Structure for Consistency

Reporting on cybersecurity within an organization takes on different meanings depending on the recipient (e.g., board of directors, organizational chiefs, business unit leads, cybersecurity staff, incident handlers) and the reporter (e.g., chief information security officer, chief risk officer, division head, director of operations, security operations center manager, incident responder). Whichever direction the reporting is facing within the organization, the goal should be to address the real risks the organization is facing, ideally within a level of risk acceptance.

Providing a structured way to communicate, understand, and discuss cybersecurity is indispensable for consistency in reporting *over time*. Settling on a predetermined structure that is used each time for discussion provides a stable platform to address the various security elements relative to the observed change in risk. Not only is the content of the reporting consequential to decision-making, but the context is also vital to understanding where key risks exist.

This is where strategic measures are taken into account. Establishing a set of key measures presented in such a way that underpins the ability to measure progress and assign accountability supports the ability to make decisions while understanding the risk implications. The implementation of key risk measures should include the main focus areas along the broad functions being measured for risk (i.e., along the chosen framework) and include no more than 15 comprehensive measures in order to maintain focus on the main risk areas, as a starting point.

Overall reporting can start with risk context—arguably, the "why are we talking about this?" level-setting discussion. Offering a view of the current threat landscape for a given quarter and how an incident resulting from these threats could have impacted the organization—based on current controls and service maturity—may provide a strong context for program-related activities.

The remaining content of the report can address the concerns of the audience. Sometimes this means offering a current view of a cyber program performance based on measures. Other times this means diving into specific risks and how the organization is addressing them. For illustrative purposes, Chapter 8 outlines a possible board report structure to address the risks faced by the organization.

There are three points to keep in mind when developing a cybersecurity board report:

- What key risks should the board be aware of at a high level every quarter? What should they be offered deeper insight into (e.g., what is the trend over time?)?

- How do these risks align with the strategic initiatives of the organization?

- What is your opinion? What do you recommend?

Remember, the board typically needs to understand or make key decisions presented to them. These decisions should come with options and implications for each option and a clear recommendation on what to do. When it comes to board reporting, one area of insight is typically challenging to communicate: how the organization compares with others in the industry. This is where discussion with others is helpful prior to presenting to the board.

Allow Measures to Mature Over Time

Two distinctive problems typically surface when exploring measures for the first time. The first is developing a top key risk measure that does not have supporting data within the organization. The second is developing a middle-to-low measure that has supporting data but does not completely address the risk.

First, simply not having the data to calculate a measure is no reason not to measure the risk. Many organizations choose to set a top key measure that is not measurable now but becomes a goal to achieve over time, largely to not lose sight of the objective. These typically are aspirational measures, setting an organizational ambition for the cybersecurity program to report on over time. In the presence of an aspirational measure, many organizations set an interim measure that may be used in its place, temporarily, until the data is available to calculate the proper value. This provides an incentive to identify, collect, and refine the data to calculate the aspirational risk measure.

Recall the "% of assets identified as critical" measure. To complete the calculation, determine the total number of assets as needed and the total number of critical assets. Yet, many organizations do not have a robust, or mature, asset management system to know either of these values. This inability to populate a risk measure indicates that the organization does not have a clear view of organizational critical assets. When this is the case, some leaders choose to stick with the aspirational measure, apply resources to address it over time, and choose a performance measure around achieving values for the measure, for example, "% completeness of asset management." This has the effect of providing insights into strategic risk reduction for the program. The sheer presence of the measure sets an intent, and that intent should align with the program's overall mission.

To address the second, many choose to drop the measure and measure something narrower and less holistically critical. For example, the "% of assets identified as critical" measure may lead some leaders to choose an interim measure of the number of applications with customer data. This interim measure may be useful for showing progress and providing step-by-step incentives for a cybersecurity team to achieve. (Note that this is where management perception is critical. Understanding what a team needs to stay motivated over time is critical in progressing against a hard topic of measuring cybersecurity risk for the first time.) Setting the aspirational measures aside until interim measures are achieved can demonstrate prerequisite progress toward addressing the broader risk. Either way, the overall intent should again align with the overall mission of the program.

What the organization chooses to measure, interim or aspirational, helps expose the organization's risk tolerance or acceptable level of risk. These measures help define tolerance by providing risk reduction decision support, even without authoritatively communicating the risk level.

Keep in Mind: Consider the Insights

Once a cybersecurity program is in place and measures begin to mature over time, the organization may experience the benefits of real risk insights. What should begin to emerge over time is not a robust measures-driven, risk reduction cybersecurity program, but rather a way of understanding cybersecurity program value. This wisdom drives where to invest and why. That is, a triumphant cybersecurity program does not meet all its measures. Rather, it provides insights into knowing where the risk is and knowing where and when to raise the bar so that attackers go away. Something akin to a "dollars for adversarial impact" starts to emerge, and questions become crisp with targeted answers; for example, should we invest in a tool that satisfies data loss or in a capability that completely stops the adversary from gaining access?

With insights into the threat landscape and wisdom from working the cybersecurity program, key insights become support for the decision, and the ability to think ahead of the risk becomes possible. One way to test these insights is to investigate the tools that the organization is considering. After working with a cybersecurity program, it should become clear that adversaries know the commercial tools. This means attackers can get around them.

Having this type of insight begins to drive decisions toward investing in a custom tool that an attacker does not know, and therefore cannot be tested against for avoidance, for protecting the valuable. The trade-offs become clearer: investing in a canned solution or building a custom solution depends on the level of security necessary for the value.

Recent Examples

Example 1. Simple Measures, Anyone?

Let's continue with the example organization where the CISO and team had a strong case to move forward with measures. The fundamentals of a cybersecurity program were in place, and the CEO was happy with the progress. The CEO asked the CISO to provide risk indicators for discussions around how risk was being addressed, but not too many. Recall the checklist in Figure 7-6.

☑	Define how we think of cybersecurity risk	Are we all using the same definition of cybersecurity risk across the enterprise?
☑	Know our critical assets	Are our critical assets understood within the enterprise?
☑	Establish clear cybersecurity activities	Are there appropriate cybersecurity activities in place, with people assigned, to address the risk?
☐	Set appropriate measures	Are key areas of cybersecurity risk being measured for risk decision-support?
☐	Prepare to respond	Are we, as an organization, ready to respond in the event of a "cyber" incident?
☐	Know the laws for the industry	Had legal counsel advised on the most current and appropriate care for the information we hold?

Figure 7-6. *Checklist marking the understanding and managing portions completed*

After another week of internal and external discussions, plus some problem-solving meetings around appropriate risks to measure, they determined that only seven measures would be developed and communicated to present and manage an appropriate view of risk for this new program. Figure 7-7 illustrates the seven simple measures that went to the board at the first meeting.

FUNCTION	DESCRIPTION	CATEGORIES	ACTIVITY	RISK MEASURE
IDENTIFY	Know the most critical assets	• Asset Management • Business Environment • Governance • Risk Assessment/ Strategy • Supply Chain Risk Mgmt	• Complete asset inventory • Critical services under mgmt. • Full cyber risk process in place • Approved risk tolerance • Third-party risk plan in place	% of assets identified as critical
PROTECT	Establish meaningful safeguards and behaviors around most critical information	• Access Control • Awareness and Training • Data Security • Information Protection • Maintenance • Protective Technology	• User access mgmt. in place • Implement security campaign • Static analysis in place • Secure SDLC in place • No remote maintenance • Removable media denied	% of privileged accounts are under privileged access control # of employees demonstrating poor security behavior # of 3rd party vendors with access to sensitive data
DETECT	Monitor for and discover potential cybersecurity events	• Anomalies and Events • Continuous Monitoring • Detection Processes (1) • Detection Processes (2)	• User behavior analysis • Weekly log analysis inspected • Threat feeds integrated • Network detection tool in place	(See # of employees demonstrating poor security behavior)
RESPOND	Prepare for and mitigate events	• Response Planning • Communications (internal and external) • Analysis • Mitigation • Improvements (response)	• Response plan developed • Response plan tested • TBD • TBD • TBD	# of hours to mitigate a critical threat, once detected
RECOVER	Reduce the impact and maximize recovery time	• Recovery planning • Improvements (recovery) • Communications (internal and external)	• Business Continuity plan in place • TBD • TBD	# of response plans tested under one year

Figure 7-7. *Simple measures for an initial board meeting on the new cybersecurity program*

To get here, the main driver was to decide on providing actionable information over data. They discovered a simple path to digest the data in a top-down vs. bottom-up way to report these seven risk measures. These measures worked for the entire organization, given the application of a new cybersecurity program. For the initial meeting, the team removed activities that were unmeasurable at this time. The current activities remained in place to make progress, but for board reporting, activities were kept to a minimum to focus on the key risks and avoid distractions. (Figure 7-8 illustrates the progress along with the checklist.)

165

☑	Define how we think of cybersecurity risk	Are we all using the same definition of cybersecurity risk across the enterprise?
☑	Know our critical assets	Are our critical assets understood within the enterprise?
☑	Establish clear cybersecurity activities	Are there appropriate cybersecurity activities in place, with people assigned, to address the risk?
☑	Set appropriate measures	Are key areas of cybersecurity risk being measured for risk decision-support?
☐	Prepare to respond	Are we, as an organization, ready to respond in the event of a "cyber" incident?
☐	Know the laws for the industry	Had legal counsel advised on the most current and appropriate care for the information we hold?

Figure 7-8. *Checklist with understanding, managing, and measuring completed*

Noticeably ready for the board, the CISO and team were not yet done. To truly ensure they were ready for any cybersecurity event, two predetermined activities remained: prepare to respond and know the laws for the industry. Having prepared for this since the beginning, the team knew what to do.

Activities for both developing and testing response plans before the end of the current quarter (Q3) were in place. This meant the security team had the foresight to discuss a proper response plan with legal counsel while in discussions about other initiatives. Fortunately, there was time to develop a working draft from a template when the teams were frequently meeting on the impact categories, tying in the protection of critical assets with roles who would need to be contacted in the event of an incident. The working draft became the final policy and procedure after one approval discussion with the CISO. The policy included the definition of an incident and procedures for whom to contact in the event of an incident. As a bonus, the team set aside a half-day exercise with executive leadership to run through a non-technical tabletop exercise to test the plan in a mock operation. This helped the team complete the circle of understanding, managing, and measuring and gave the executive leadership confidence that a plan was in place in the event of an incident. The CISO was able to confidently check this action complete, as Figure 7-9 illustrates.

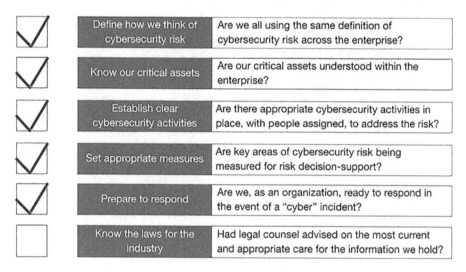

Figure 7-9. *Checklist with understanding, managing, measuring, and responding completed*

Not to be left with an incomplete list, and to be sure the organization was up to speed with the applicable laws and regulations, the CISO leaned into their last task.

With a strong relationship between the security team and legal counsel built during the critical assets and impact work accomplished to date, the legal team was deeply curious about the developing cybersecurity laws and regulations not only in the areas the company operated in currently but also where the company planned to operate in the near future.

The team was already familiar with the applicable laws and regulations for the existing business, for example, General Data Protection Regulation, US Privacy Act compliance, and Payment Card Industry compliance.

But the board had not been properly exposed to the laws and regulations, and certainly not in the context of what the organization was prepared to do to ensure compliance. The result was an overview as part of the upcoming board discussion. Figure 7-10 illustrates the synthesized version of two laws used for a board-level discussion.

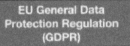

EU General Data Protection Regulation (GDPR)	Privacy Act
GDPR requires entities operating in the EU to adhere to specific data subject (i.e., EU citizen) protections - Entities "passing certain thresholds should be mandated to appoint a Data Protection Officer" - Requires covered entities to report breach notification within 72 hours of "first having become aware of the breach" - Entities reaching the GDPR may be fined up to 4% of annual global revenue or €20 Million (whichever is greater) - Replaces the Data Protection Directive 95/46/EC	The Privacy Act of 1974 (5 U.S.C. § 552a) governs the collection, use, and dissemination of a record about an individual maintained by federal agencies - Prohibits the disclosure of any record maintained in a system of records to any person or agency without the written consent of the record subject; statutory exceptions exist - Provides legal remedies that permit an individual to seek enforcement of the rights granted under the act

Figure 7-10. *Two of the laws (at the time) applicable to this organization*

Overall, the CISO and team had tenuously run through the fundamental components for creating a sustainable cybersecurity program. As the CISO marked off the final checkbox on the checklist in Figure 7-11, they were now prepared to report up to the board and start the journey of maturing a functioning cybersecurity risk reduction program.

✓	Define how we think of cybersecurity risk	Are we all using the same definition of cybersecurity risk across the enterprise?
✓	Know our critical assets	Are our critical assets understood within the enterprise?
✓	Establish clear cybersecurity activities	Are there appropriate cybersecurity activities in place, with people assigned, to address the risk?
✓	Set appropriate measures	Are key areas of cybersecurity risk being measured for risk decision-support?
✓	Prepare to respond	Are we, as an organization, ready to respond in the event of a "cyber" incident?
✓	Know the laws for the industry	Had legal counsel advised on the most current and appropriate care for the information we hold?

Figure 7-11. *A completed checklist for starting a cybersecurity program*

Example 2. Too Much Data, Not Enough Information

A very large organization in the transportation sector was struggling to get everyone on the same page for appropriate cyber measures to bring to the board of directors. As a highly regulated industry, they had access to and robust analysis from large sets of data; however, they were unable to pull it together to provide enough information on the overall organization.

After years of digesting a "metric ton" of data, they decided this was a top-down problem (strategy) vs. a bottom-up problem (tactical). To solve it, they started with the fundamentals.

First, they settled on what they were doing (understanding the risk). Using a known framework, attention went to a top-down view of their risks and their mission in the cybersecurity program, which was to "deliver a security program to reduce critical data loss." The overall objective was to identify risk in a way that "makes sense to the enterprise."

With this understanding, they structured the main outcomes they wanted at the end of this effort:

- Meet regulators' demands. Provide a broad set of values for what the company is doing to what regulators need.

- Educate the board on what the company is doing to reduce the risk. Help them understand the risk so that it may be mitigated.

- Communicate the value of the programs addressing the risk through meaningful value.

With this scope, they set out to quantify uncertainty in a way that provides decision-makers the appropriate level of risk mitigation and coverage through measurement. They understood that good measures mature over time, as the organization better understands its cybersecurity posture: a large lesson from measuring performance in transportation. So they began by asking some questions within the organization:

- What information is relevant/helpful?

- What can they measure?

- What is acceptable?

- How does it relate to the health of the enterprise?

When general but substantial answers came back, they probed a bit deeper and asked this question: if they were to provide meaningful measures of risk and maturity, which values would speak to actionable risk reduction? The following is what came back:

- **Risk reduction** (e.g., elapsed time to respond, elapsed time to discover), ones that speak to the business units and would get them involved in the process.

- **Organizational cyber practices** (e.g., employees practicing poor cybersecurity, mean time to patch unpatched systems[4]).

- **Those who bring risks into the organization** (e.g., number of third-party vendors with access to sensitive data and use of that data).

- **Ability to respond to realized risks** (e.g., the time between detection and response).

- **Ability to respond to an event** (e.g., number of response plans tested over one year). This way, they made sure not to over-emphasize on only one risk function, like detection, and overlook proper risk, like the ability to recover from a catastrophic event.

They next defined where to get the data, which was a less challenging task now that specific values were sought after. At the end of the effort, they landed on seven measures that worked for the entire organization that looked like Figure 7-12.

FUNCTION	DESCRIPTION	...	..	RISK MEASURE
IDENTIFY	Know the most critical assets	...	...	% of assets identified as critical
PROTECT	Establish meaningful safeguards and behaviors around most critical information	...	...	# of employees demonstrating poor security behavior # (mean) time to patch # of 3rd party vendors with access to sensitive data
DETECT	Monitor for and discover potential cybersecurity events	...	...	# time from discovered threat to response team activity
RESPOND	Prepare for and mitigate events	...	...	# time to mitigate a critical threat, once detected
RECOVER	Reduce the impact and maximize recovery time	...	...	# of response plans tested under one year

Figure 7-12. *Seven measures of risk that worked for the organization*

---

[4] The value for "mean time to patch" was calculated as (1) the date from when vulnerability is publicly known (+2) to the time when the vulnerability is patched (/3) all the patches across the enterprise over a rolling 12-month period.

Overall, they got comfortable with the one approach and became focused on what they were not measuring (e.g., the difference between incident and response), setting the stage for maturing measures over time.

Throughout this process, the team learned a few key lessons:

- **Start with one approach**. Get comfortable with one approach, but be prepared to accept what is not being measured now. Once the measurement process starts, insights on what is missing become clear—in this case, for example, measuring the difference between incident and response.

- **Understand which problem is being solved.** Understanding the problem being solved is critical. If not well understood, the ability to effectively manage, measure, and mitigate is compromised.

- **Get feedback**. Boards are requesting risk reduction measures in support of overall organizational objectives. Anticipating or figuring out what to measure and report requires a lot of insights and integration into the overall business. Feedback from business units is essential to ensuring that the information is accurate and that the people have a pathway back to the top to report challenges in the data.

Pitfalls to Avoid

Choosing the right measures matters. The main pitfall to avoid is the lack of a strategy behind what is being measured (i.e., the inability to link a measure to a plan or determine the expected value) to provide insights. It should always be clear what value is now and where it needs to be in the future. Overall, following a plan should help avoid other common pitfalls.

The following are some common pitfalls:

- **Pitfall 1**: Choosing non-insightful measures (e.g., how many DDoS attacks, how many incidents). It is a good risk context but not a measure of risk management.

- **Pitfall 2**: Choosing static measures that do not mature over time (i.e., setting a measure that only tells one part of the story, or "setting and forgetting"). Measures should improve as you improve. For example, take measures to a risk committee or peers that report on compliance for risk management. Starting there can help report what is needed now and then fine-tune some of the measures over time.

- **Pitfall 3**: Confusing the difference between tactical and strategic measures. Failing to pull back and view the organizational risk from a top-down view can quickly pull teams into the deeply tactical. Strategic measures should support the overall strategy and be supported by bottom-up measures.

CHAPTER 8

Report Upward

Introduction

Providing information and insights that allow for a sufficient level of oversight relative to the business's operations is the main goal of reporting upward.

"How do I report to the board?" This is a common question in the cybersecurity community. It should have one simple answer: whatever the board requests. However, it's not that simple. Many board members are unclear about what questions to ask in cybersecurity. It should be expected that each board member has a different level of cybersecurity understanding from the next; naturally, each member of a board typically has deep expertise in functional areas that are not fundamentally cybersecurity. This means that many board members neither have deep technical knowledge nor deep information security experience required to dive deep into relevant technical cybersecurity problems... and this is usually by design. What board members do have is a reason for being on the board, relevant to the other board members in support of the organizational strategy. This role comes with clarity on the duties of the board—one of which being risk oversight. With this in mind, the question "How do I report to the board?" might be answered this way: whatever the board needs to know to provide a sufficient level of oversight.

This answer may not be as pragmatic as one would like, but it is straightforward. Recall that what an organization chooses to measure in cybersecurity indicates the level at which the security problem is understood, for example, measuring the number of DDoS/phishing attacks as a "risk" rather than the number of employees demonstrating poor security behavior. This applies chiefly to board reporting, as the board is consuming strategic measures that should quantify uncertainty in a manner that provides decision-makers the appropriate level of insights for risk mitigation and impact. If the overall objective of a cybersecurity risk program is to anticipate and mitigate cybersecurity risk, then the reporting on that program should communicate the current and future states of the program so that the risk is understood well enough to provide sufficient risk oversight. If not, there is a breakdown in overall cybersecurity risk management.

At the strategic level, reporting on the cybersecurity program should take the whole organization into account. Similar to a financial health check on any organization, reporting on a cybersecurity program should provide a point-in-time update on the organization's cybersecurity risk.

Rules to Follow

Recall from Chapter 7 the three questions to keep in mind when developing a cybersecurity board report:

- What are the key risks and trends the board should be aware of (at a high level), and what risks require deeper insight?

- How do these risks impact organizational strategic initiatives?

- What is your opinion? What do you recommend?

These three questions should be kept in mind before jumping into the rules for reporting to the board.

Rules to Follow: Report Upward

The following are the four basic rules in reporting:

- **Rule 1:** Choose a consistent reporting structure.

- **Rule 2:** Provide clear and informative measures.

- **Rule 3:** Use straightforward terms.

- **Rule 4:** Provide recommendations for all problems.

Choose a Consistent Reporting Structure

When it comes to the reporting structure, consistency matters. Board members are not involved in the day-to-day operations of the organization. Typically, the board will not have had much communication on cybersecurity since the last report; not all discussions with the CEO and other key organizational leaders revolve around cybersecurity.[1] Maintaining a consistent structure helps demonstrate progress over time.

Board reports are typically shaped by the board and the chief (e.g., CEO, president). A common preliminary cybersecurity structure is outlined in Figure 8-1.

---

[1] Unless, of course, there is a cybersecurity incident in the news. Newsworthy events typically get a lot of attention by board members to best understand the fundamental issues of the recent incident as well as how it may apply to the organization.

How to: Build out an initial Board report

To begin structuring a first board report, address a few key topics:

- Current "**Threat Landscape**" for a given quarter and how that incident could have impacted our organization based on current controls and service maturity.
  - O Informing as to what cyber threats have impacted the world in the previous quarter
  - O Current organizational posture against known incident findings
- Current "**Cyber Program Performance**" measures. Measures against the overall Risk Management Program -- tracking on multi-year InfoSec strategy roadmap and its progress. This may include such topics as:
  - O Key InfoSec service metrics in-line with how it's managed (e.g., framework)
  - O Tracking on InfoSec service maturity
  - O Overview of cost per control area and the estimated impact in risk reduction it offers (Note: security controls often lack a true ROI but a Risk Reduction measure based on the investment type may help in the calculation to show value of investments);
  - O Annual review and approval for certain categories
  - O Findings from Internal Audits/Pen-Tests/Fed exams/SEC Exams
  - O Trending from weekly SOC reports and what they mean for the organization

---

- The "**ask**" (if requesting or justifying resources)
  - O Prioritized view of the requests, based on impact to the organization
  - O Changes to program
  - O Budget increase explanations
- A "**learning**" moment (possibly lead-in for next quarter).
  - O Recurring quarterly topics and ad-hoc "big rocks" for the InfoSec program expected to equate to moderate to significant risk reduction

---

Figure 8-1. *Outline for an initial board report on cybersecurity*

Again, board reports are typically shaped by what the CEO or president needs to communicate, but providing insights that address the business's operations also carries significant value.

Provide Clear and Informative Measures

All boards are different, and each individual board has a collectively different level of cybersecurity awareness based on actual board members. From a risk point of view, it is important to develop a professional relationship with the board that enables a transparent discussion around the topic of risk. Perhaps this presents an opportunity to educate the board on what is being done to reduce the risk—in other words, an opportunity to help them understand the risk, so that it may be mitigated. For example, are there risks to address to meet regulators' demands? If so, addressing regulation may be an opportunity to champion the adoption of a common risk framework to act as a *translation table* to map what the organization is doing to what regulators need.

For measures, it is important to provide a clear view of what is being measured and why. Board-level metrics are *strategic*, supported by tactical measures. Operational, or tactical, measures can be used to support the overall strategic measures if needed. Otherwise, consider leaving the tactical to the management discussions following the meeting—mainly to avoid distracting from the larger, strategic, points of the discussion.

Providing a clear view of what is being measured and why helps frame the conversation for insights into the measures and the changing risk landscape. One of the ways to provide insights is to report on certain trends over time. For example, measures supplemented with a directional trendline (e.g., upward, flat, downward) can provide context on program efficiency or effectiveness, such as the impact certain programs are having on risk mitigation. With a particular goal, or objective, for the measures, adding a simple trendline can help communicate the direction the risk is taking, relative to what is being measured. Figure 8-2 illustrates a simple way to communicate these trends, borrowing measures from Chapter 7.

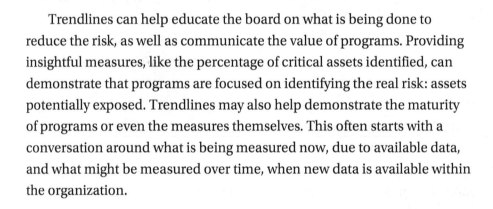

Figure 8-2. *Illustrative measures with trends for reporting on cybersecurity*

Trendlines can help educate the board on what is being done to reduce the risk, as well as communicate the value of programs. Providing insightful measures, like the percentage of critical assets identified, can demonstrate that programs are focused on identifying the real risk: assets potentially exposed. Trendlines may also help demonstrate the maturity of programs or even the measures themselves. This often starts with a conversation around what is being measured now, due to available data, and what might be measured over time, when new data is available within the organization.

Keep in Mind: Consider the Value

Note that the resource investment in measures should be less than the return from measures. Choose informative measures that provide actionable feedback across the organization and mature over time. That is, measure what can be measured now, focusing on what might be measured later. For example, *the number of employees demonstrating poor security behavior* might start as a measure of how many people fail phishing campaigns and later mature to include employees who fail more than once or trigger a data loss event.

The goal is not necessarily to be compliant with a risk concept, but rather the ability to measure the level of maturity needed just above what attackers need to impact certain parts of the organization. At some point in reporting on cybersecurity, the value comes down to "dollars for adversarial impact." This means understanding the tradeoff between investing in a tool that addresses one narrow technical threat or investing in an architeture that stops most threats from gaining access to cricial assets. Mature programs—and, thus, program reporting—consider the value of investments relative to what the attacker will spend to defeat that investment. Tools, as purchased activities or investments, illustrate this point best: most commercially available cybersecurity tools are known by attackers, and attackers know how to get around them. Mature programs consider the value when making decisions. For example, should the organization invest in a commercial solution or a custom solution? Answers depend on the level of security deemed necessary for the value.

Use Straightforward Terms

Technology is increasingly becoming more and more complex. Before reporting upward to executives or management, run through a communication test: can you explain your point in two sentences?

Keep practicing until you can.

Boards typically are not technical experts. They don't need to be. They need to know the maturity level and fundamental challenges in how the organization understands and manages cybersecurity risk. The less technical and more reasonable the language is when communicating cybersecurity risk, the easier it is to understand the problem being solved and the solutions for solving it. There is enough complexity in cybersecurity, and using straightforward terms helps reduce that complexity so the main goal may stay in focus: the ability to quantify uncertainty in a way that provides decision-makers the appropriate level of risk mitigation and coverage.

Provide Recommendations for All Problems

Problems without recommendations are expressed problems with no clear solutions. One pitfall to avoid in reporting upward is offering problems that have no solution, possible solution, or expert point of view on a solution. All problems need a resolution option when reporting upward, even if the solution is to understand the problem better. Possible solutions do not have to be perfect, but they do need to be insightful and have an accompanying point of view from the person closest to the problem.

Insights gleaned from in-use measures can help in sticky situations where problems seem to have no apparent solution. The in-use measures represent a current understanding of the cybersecurity program. Using them can provide context for how problems may have impact, or implications, on other parts of the organization. Clarity is essential when communicating risks to the organization. To properly address the risks, each problem should have a recommendation. One way to string these points together using an incident response team availability problem may be as follows: (1) resource constraints are reducing the ability to respond to incidents; (2) lack of an incident response team increases the financial loss to the business during an incident; and (3) an investment of x in two incident responders should reduce our potential loss of y during an actual incident

Pitfalls to Avoid

Reporting upward has its challenges. Avoiding some pitfalls may make it easier. Similar to measures, the main pitfall to avoid in upward communication is the lack of a strategy behind reporting. The inability to link what is being reported to an overall strategic plan provides no insights to the board. The plan should always be clear.

The following are common pitfalls of first-time board reporting:

- **Pitfall 1**: Turning the boardroom into a problem-solving session without all the facts.

- **Pitfall 2**: A lack of clear recommendations or options with risk implications for presented decisions.

- **Pitfall 3**: Over-indexing a tactical solution or problem without addressing the board's strategic implication.

- **Pitfall 4**: Not understanding how the organization compares with others.

CHAPTER 9

Questions Boards Should Ask

Introduction

ABSTRACT

Boards may ask a set of non-technical yet probing questions to ascertain the maturity level of the way an organization understands and manages cybersecurity risk.

Boards of directors do not need to be technical experts to oversee or discover cybersecurity risks in organizations. However, they need to ask probing questions to ascertain the maturity level and fundamental challenges in the way the organization understands and manages cybersecurity risk. There is only one fact they do need to know: the ability to compromise any organization is possible because nothing is truly secure.

Executive boards of directors, M&A due diligence analysts, and venture capital investors all want to know what questions need to be asked to get a sense of the real cybersecurity risks within an organization.

One answer is relatively straightforward but not always obvious: ask probing questions about the overall organizational approach to cyber risk, and seek evidence of measurable facts supporting that approach. This may sound fundamental and non-technical. Well, it *is* fundamental and non-technical.

© Ryan Leirvik 2023
R. Leirvik, *Understand, Manage, and Measure Cyber Risk*,
https://doi.org/10.1007/978-1-4842-9319-5_9

The impact of a cyber incident can vary by organization, and with that variation, so does the relative cybersecurity risk. Operational impacts, reputational impacts, legal impacts, and even licensing impacts are typically different between organizations. They are highly dependent on the type of business, governance of data/systems, and severity of a cybersecurity incident.

Many organizations speak about controls, technical fixes, expert people, and technical tools to address this risk. These tactical solutions solve particular risk management problems, like blocking, monitoring, detection, and remediation. While greatly important, these solutions do not solve the oversight problems concerning directors or potential investors.

The problem for directors or investors is to determine the overall organizational cyber maturity relative to the risk. What is that level of maturity, and has the enterprise identified its real risk of a cyber incident? The board (particularly) and investors (generally) have an oversight problem to solve, not a management problem.

This leads back to the beginning: What questions do I need to ask to get a sense of the real cybersecurity risk within an organization? In essence, where do I start?

To quickly examine the organizational thinking and fundamental management in cybersecurity, here are five questions to get the discussions going as part of overnight or any due diligence[1]:

01.   *What do you perceive as your cybersecurity risk?*

This question probes for a direct answer to an intentionally broad and open-ended question. You don't need to know, or even judge, the merit of any

---

[1] Note this is a starting point. Mature organizations will have detailed and well-defined answers to these simple questions. When that is the case, things are off to a good start, and you have enough to frame a point of view on the overall organizational cybersecurity.

answer, but you do need to judge the organization's ability to provide a sufficient answer. The answer to this question provides a view into the organizational thinking about cybersecurity risk. The following are examples:

- Is there an understanding of both the probability and real impact of an incident? (Examples include potential costs for a particular type of cybercrime, fines related to the loss of specific types of data, and potential revenue loss related to a reputational impact.)

- How likely is a type of breach to occur? (Which threats are most concerning or most likely to be successful? Which vulnerabilities related to these threats are known and not properly addressed?)

- What happens to the organization when specific risks are realized? (What are the legal duties? Who are the response leaders? What are the recovery plans?)

02. *How are you managing this risk?*

This question takes a deeper look into the perceived, or known, risk to examine the organizational thinking and structural alignment supporting cyber risk mitigation. Knowing what an enterprise cybersecurity risk management program looks like (e.g., frameworks, risk-mitigating controls, roles and responsibilities, training) is not as important—from an oversight perspective—as obtaining evidence that a program is in place. The exact framework,[2] approach, or structure taken by an organization is less important (at this stage) as the simple fact that a thought-out risk management approach is in place. For example, you might look for the following:

- A structured way to address cyber risk management that helps understand and address the actual cybersecurity risks faced by the organization

- Evidence of cyber risk management nested within a larger enterprise risk management framework (e.g., cybersecurity incident response plans referenced in global business continuity planning)

- The use of an applicable cybersecurity risk management framework (e.g., NIST Cybersecurity Framework, ISO/IEC 27K, Open Worldwide Application Security Project® (OWASP), Factor Analysis of Information Risk (FAIR) framework, the NIST 800 Series, MITRE ATT&CK, AuditScripts Critical Security Controls)

03. *How are you measuring the reduction of cybersecurity risk?*

Brace yourself. This question pokes right into the widely contested and heavily uncertain subject of measuring risk. (Note: Tread lightly, and look for areas to provide oversight and guidance where

---

[2] Any one framework does not match any one organization. Which framework chosen by an organization is less important than when a framework (or frameworks) was (were) chosen, from an oversight point of view.

answers fall short of sufficient.) The concept and relative meaningfulness of *cyber risk metrics* introduce their own investigation.

From an oversight or potential investment perspective, what is being measured is not as important as the meaningfulness (to you, the immediate risk examiner) of the organizational action that may be taken from the result of the measurements. Overall, you are looking for the ability to identify, address, and adapt to the appropriate level of risk governance and oversight: that is, the organizational cyber risk policy and overall risk appetite.[3]

What an organization measures in cybersecurity indicates the level at which they view the security problem. This topic leads to a much wider discussion on the use and value of KRIs, KPIs, and metrics; consider listening for evidence of two concepts:

- Is the objective to quantify uncertainty in a way that provides decision-makers the appropriate level of risk mitigation and coverage through measurement?

- Is it understood that meaningful measures mature over time as the organization better understands its cybersecurity posture? (No measurement is perfect, especially at its onset.)

---

[3] Risk appetite is the level of known risk an organization is willing to... err... stomach.

04. *Who owns cybersecurity risk management within the organization?*

This is the cybersecurity roles-and-responsibilities question. Here, you are asking a very specific question: *when it comes to cybersecurity, who has the lead?*[4]

There should be a clear distinction between who owns the *risk* and who owns the *management of the risk*. That is, the organization is accountable for the risk, but someone has the responsibility for managing it, transparently. Up to this point, you have investigated the organizational alignment to the cyber risk problem and discovered how the cybersecurity risk responsibilities are structured within the organization (i.e., how cyber risk management may roll up from IT controls to you, the overseer/investor). Now it's prudent to identify the lead.

First, "everyone" is not an answer—from an oversight perspective, we know that "everyone" equals "no one." Answers to this question should provide clarity. The following are some examples:

- Is there a clear information security risk management owner in the organization? (This may be a CISO, CRO, or information security manager.)

---

[4] Typically, the organization, or the organization's chief, has the responsibility of aptly balancing the risk, where the CISO, CRO, or information security manager helps the organization understand and manage the risk. True risk "ownership" typically is an organizational decision.

- Where are the organizational incentives to maintain risk mitigation solutions in place? That is, does the owner have a strategic direction for operational control over critical assets (i.e., data or systems considered critical to be kept safe/undisturbed) to avoid costly organizational impact?

- Are crisis-driven roles assigned, or do pre-assigned roles and responsibilities exist?

This leads to the fifth and final question you should ask.

05. *How are you prepared to respond to a cybersecurity incident?*

Arguably, the previous four questions have led to this main takeaway. Here, you are questioning the readiness to respond if an incident happens.

An organization's ability to respond to an incident may be the predominant issue a board or an investor needs to know. How an organization responds to a cybersecurity incident/issue can increase or decrease the severity of that incident and, therefore, the impact. There are several areas to probe, but response readiness in any organization may ultimately come down to the following:

- Pre-assigned roles and responsibilities by title for incident response (do the people who need to act know what to do?).

- Strategic alignment to a communications plan, in case of an emergency.

- Identification (ideally classification) of critical assets within the organization—this helps clarify the impact and identify who needs to know (e.g., legal authorities, customers, executives).

- One point of contact for command and control over the response effort.

With answers to these five questions, you should have a sense of organizational thinking around addressing cybersecurity risk in non-technical terms. Ideally, one will obtain measurable facts to support risk management. These questions, although relatively straightforward, are not always obvious and may provide a simple way to understand how an organization is thinking about the impact of cybersecurity risk.

A Tear Sheet for Boards

Five questions for discovering fundamental challenges in the way organizations manage cybersecurity risk are addressed in Figure 9-1.

(1) Understanding: What is your cybersecurity risk?	
Concerning Indicators:	Encouraging Indicators:
• Narrow view of cybersecurity risk, or impact limited to non-critical operations	• Identification or knowledge of **critical data or systems** requiring protection from an organizational level
• Uncertainty around the topic or the actual problem being solved, such as a laundry list of "cyber" activities lacking a strategic approach or a clear narrative	• Thoughtfulness around the **relevance** of threats and **likelihood of impact** to the organization (e.g., legal fines related to data loss, recovery cost estimates, potential revenue impact)
(2) Managing: How are you managing cybersecurity risk?	
Concerning Indicators:	Encouraging Indicators:
• Heavy focus on technical controls out-of-context with an applicable risk management framework	• A **clear management structure and framework** to address organizational cybersecurity risk management (e.g., NIST CSF, OWASP, FIAR, MITRE ATT&CK™)
• Complicated and unsystematic risk-management approach(es), or overreliance on a one-size-fits-all "cybersecurity program"	• A cybersecurity risk management program nested within a larger **enterprise risk management plan** (e.g., cybersecurity incident response plans referenced in global business continuity planning)
(3) Measuring: How are you measuring cybersecurity risk reduction?	
Concerning Indicators:	Encouraging Indicators:
• Clear, crisp, authoritative measures of *factual-but-uninformative* data (e.g., number of DDoS/phishing attacks)	• Heavy debate on **informative measures** of cybersecurity risk relative to the *organization*
• Over-reliance on audits and compliance-driven data reviews	• Actionable management gaps (e.g., time from discovered threat to response team activity)
• Deference to technical experts for explanations of what is measured	• Addressable management activities (e.g., number of employees demonstrating poor security behavior)
(4) Structuring: Who owns cybersecurity risk within the organization?	
Concerning Indicators:	Encouraging Indicators:
• Split authority across cybersecurity (e.g., CRO owns information protection while CISO/CIO owns protection technology)	• Clear **structural through-line** from executive management to operations in support of organizational cybersecurity risk mitigation
• Routinely shifting responsibility and internal lines of communication	• Organizational ownership or **operational control over "critical" assets** like data or systems considered critical
(5) Responding: How are you prepared to respond to a cybersecurity incident?	
Concerning Indicators:	Encouraging Indicators:
• Crisis-assigned roles and responsibilities individual (e.g., line-of-site tasking)	• Pre-assigned roles and responsibilities established by title for incident response
• Ambiguous/unreachable point-of-contact for response effort	• Reasonable cadence for practicing a response (e.g., tabletop exercises each year/quarter)

Figure 9-1. *Five questions for discovering fundamental challenges in the way organizations manage cybersecurity risk*

Boards of directors and investors do not need to be technical experts to oversee or discover cybersecurity risks in organizations. However, they need to ask probing questions to ascertain the maturity level of, and fundamental challenges within, the way organizations understand and manage cybersecurity risk.

CHAPTER 10

Conclusion

Introduction

ABSTRACT

Most organizations rely on imperfect information technology (IT) to enable business and operational functions. These imperfections expose attractive perforations for some unauthorized users. Understanding what these users are after and what is critical to the business is vital for getting a handle on cybersecurity risk management. With that handle, a management approach may be put into place and supported by proper measures that quantify uncertainty as uncertainty changes. These basic foundational components help focus attention and resources for organizational management: the ability to understand, manage, and properly measure cybersecurity risk.

Reducing organizational cybersecurity risk while simultaneously keeping up with the business is a challenge for many organizations. When addressing cybersecurity, some basic foundational components can help focus attention and organize around the ability to understand, manage, and properly measure cybersecurity risk.

First, Understand the Risk

What problem are you solving?

Understanding the complexities of cybersecurity can be challenging. Without first being clear about the actual risk problem, many organizations struggle to effectively solve it by deploying a sufficient risk-mitigating

© Ryan Leirvik 2023
R. Leirvik, *Understand, Manage, and Measure Cyber Risk*,
https://doi.org/10.1007/978-1-4842-9319-5_10

cybersecurity program. The program-supporting functions of program management and proper measurement begin to fail, as the risk is simply not well understood at the program level and certainly not well understood across the key organizational areas of the organization, such as management, technology, and executive oversight. Programs lacking a sharply articulated view of the risk lose out on the benefits of an objective-based program, such as a long-term view of risk, insights into actual organizational risk tolerance, gaps in program controls, and appropriate measures for the board of directors.

One simple way to address this challenge is to properly define *risk* first. Then inventory and categorize organizational assets so that the most valuable assets may be identified based on the overall impact to the organization when the confidentiality, integrity, or availability of the asset is compromised.

Recall that virtually all technology used in business contains unintended flaws. These flaws reside in convenient and inconvenient places, are intended or unintended, and take on many sizes and shapes. Recall that the underlying IT design and networking that made software and hardware function properly were not built with malicious use in mind.[1] Also, recall that untrustworthy groups and individuals exist in the world, seeking to do harm to others or achieve some sort of gainful advantage. All of this is to say that the use of technology introduces unintended risks to every institution. Understanding the risks in underlying technology means gaining clarity on the real risk to the overall organization.

Generating one common definition of risk is a good place to start when tackling what risk to acknowledge. This clear definition of cybersecurity risk should fit inside the organization's overall risk management; that is, risk within the organization should all fit together in some common way.

---

[1] Designing with security in mind and "security as design" are still relatively new concepts, as individuals and organizations have taken advantage of an inherent trust model.

For cybersecurity, a definition that clearly articulates the risk is the most helpful. One resource to turn to for a definition is NISTIR 762r1. This helpful reference points out ways in defining cybersecurity threats, vulnerabilities, and risks to the enterprise that are easy to communicate. For example, "risk is a function of threats, vulnerabilities, the likelihood of an event, and the potential impact such an event would have to the [organization]" brings clarity to typically unclear areas when working with others outside of information security. Figure 10-1 is an illustrative diagram of cybersecurity risk adopted from this definition.

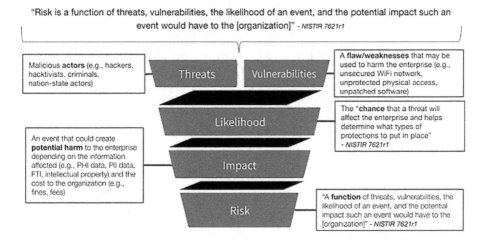

Figure 10-1. *Defining cybersecurity risk using NISTIR 7621r1*

Starting with a clear definition of cybersecurity risk arms organizational leadership with a grasp on how the risk may manifest itself inside the organization, for example, a specific attacker using a vulnerability to drive down the organizational reputation. By understanding risk, information security teams and leaders can recognize what is *critical* within the organization. They need to identify all assets that would significantly impact core objectives should they escape, be tampered with, or be used in an unauthorized manner. A clear definition of *critical* helps turn the focus toward what is *dire*, or most valuable, to the organization, providing a focal point for what makes up an actual critical asset.

Defining the term *critical* for the organization is an essential prerequisite for managing the risk; after all, it is a fundamental component to understanding exactly what needs to be properly managed to avoid the impact on the organization. When defining what is critical, taking the attacker's perspective is a useful way to help distinguish between what is useful inside the company and what might be useful outside the company. To help further this distinction for critical and non-critical assets, some organizations find it helpful to categorize these views into three different viewpoints:

- **Inside-out**: What do internal employees believe to be critical? Tally or categorize each asset and then ask the following question: how do these assets contribute to the core mission? It should be apparent that not all assets are sensitive enough to significantly impact the business if affected. These are not critical.

- **Outside-in**: What might attackers/adversaries find valuable? Tally or categorize each asset valuable to an attacker, and then ask this question: what harm would come if an attacker successfully gained access to these assets? These are the critical asset classes.

- **Organizational**: Apply an organizational risk focus to what is truly critical. If lost or tampered with, which assets will harm the organization in terms of reputation, revenue, or costs? These are the *critical assets*, and they need constant, successful defense.

This may help define critical as something akin to "assets that will significantly impact the core objectives should the assets escape, be tampered with, or be used in an unauthorized manner."

With a point of view on the term *critical*, the process of pinpointing what is and what is not critical becomes a bit easier. This process begins with an inventory of assets (one of the most imperative endeavors for any IT progress). An organization needs to know what technology property exists so that the most valuable may be identified and, ideally, protected. One way to do this is to frame and complete a simple worksheet like the one shown in Figure 10-2.

ASSET CLASS	DEFINITION	ASSET	ASSET ID	LOCATION	OWNER
DEVICES	Exact meaning of "Devices"	• TBD • TBD • TBD	• D-1 • D-2 • D-3	• LOC • LOC • LOC	• TITLE • TITLE • TITLE
APPLICATIONS	Exact meaning of "Applications"	• TBD • TBD • TBD	• A-1 • A-2 • A-3	• LOC • LOC • LOC	• TITLE • TITLE • TITLE
NETWORKS	Exact meaning of "Networks"	• TBD • TBD • TBD	• N-1 • N-2 • N-3	• LOC • LOC • LOC	• TITLE • TITLE • TITLE
DATA	Exact meaning of "Data"	• TBD • TBD • TBD	• DA-1 • DA-2 • DA-3	• LOC • LOC • LOC	• TITLE • TITLE • TITLE
USERS	Exact meaning of "Users"	• TBD • TBD • TBD	• U-1 • U-2 • U-3	• LOC • LOC • LOC	• TITLE • TITLE • TITLE

Figure 10-2. *Illustrative asset inventory worksheet*

The goal is to have visibility into the type of asset, its whereabouts, and the actual owner so that proper management may be applied to each and sufficient controls presented around assets deemed critical. The central concept is to develop and maintain a satisfactory record, with responsible owners, for each asset discovered in the organization.

With a set inventory, categorizing assets becomes straightforward. For example, critical assets (e.g., data, devices, applications, networks, users) may be grouped according to the potential harm a cybersecurity event could do to organizational data (e.g., PHI data, PII data, FTI, intellectual property), devices (e.g., web cams, displays, machinery, appliances), applications (e.g., key services, software), users (e.g., employees), or resources (e.g., costs due to fines, people tied up in incident response). Pinpointing these types of potential harm-inducing organizational assets offers managers the ability to understand them and then manage them and then measure the associated risk to the business operations should these assets be compromised in some way.

Once established, the organization can develop and maintain an asset management risk register to mark and track risks to critical assets. This is where the work of clearly anticipating the risks to these organizational elements may begin. The challenge, simply put, is that the process requires both an artful and a mathematical approach to anticipating the clear impact on an organization. Far too many approaches exist to bring clarity to this problem. The central decision factor in choosing an approach should relate to how the organization has defined cybersecurity risk and the overall fidelity of risk management desired. For example, an organization that demands precision on the potential costs of a cybersecurity incident may choose quantitative measures to answer this question: how much would a breach of [specific magnitude] cost? An organization that waives the precision for a rougher estimate may opt for a qualitative approach to the same question. Either way, the risk register becomes a helpful tool in tracking and debating potential risks to each asset. Figure 10-3 is a simplified illustration of a risk register.

PRIORITY	ASSET ID	RISK	IMPACT	EXPOSURE	STATUS
1	D-1	• TBD	• TBD	H / M / L	• TBD
2	D-1	• TBD	• TBD	H / M / L	• TBD
3	D-3	• TBD	• TBD	H / M / L	• TBD
4	D-4	• TBD	• TBD	H / M / L	• TBD
5	D-5	• TBD	• TBD	H / M / L	• TBD

Figure 10-3. *A simplified illustration of a risk register*

With this, it should be clear that the risk is relative to protecting critical assets. Understanding the risk offers the ability to properly manage the risk.

Next, Manage the Risk

With time now invested in exploring and categorizing crucial organizational assets and a crisp cybersecurity goal articulated, the risk should be well understood as cybersecurity risk to critical assets. Managing that cybersecurity risk now has a better chance for success than moving forward without a clear understanding of the problem.

The starting point here is to focus on the overall cybersecurity program before jumping into managing each specific risk or set of risks. A few simple rules exist when it comes to starting a program:

- Focus on one framework to start.

- Structure the organizational management approach along the program framework.

- Set a review frequency for the overall program.

- Prepare to respond and recover from an event, as part of the program.

How an organization addresses cybersecurity is critical to reducing overall risk and mitigating the severity of any cyber incident. This means having an established, structured approach for the whole of the cybersecurity program, that is, a scaffolding for ensuring the program is broad enough to address the risks and a prescribed guide for how each risk is addressed.

The framework is a structured way to address cyber risk program management, helping understand and address cybersecurity risks faced by the organization. Many well-defined, highly useful frameworks exist for managing risk for the entire organization or enterprise. Many available cybersecurity management frameworks exist to address all types of risks at various organizational levels. Beginning with a known framework is a helpful way to shape a program to best understand the risks faced by an organization and position the organization to speak a common language across multiple industries and sectors.

Applying a framework to start keeps attention on what is at risk. For example, the National Institute of Standards and Technology (NIST) released version 1.0 of the Framework for Improving Critical Infrastructure Cybersecurity (CSF) on February 12, 2014, and an updated version 1.1 in April 2018. The CSF acts as a structured way to help understand and address cybersecurity risks faced by any organization. The CSF is built around key cybersecurity disciplines that work across any organizational size (e.g., small business, large business, enterprise) and virtually any industry (e.g., healthcare, hospitality, banking, finance, energy, or retail).

The CSF starts with the Identify function, indicating that understanding the organization's risk is driven by knowing your technology to point you to the risk. This helps drive what to measure, how to inform your strategy, how much to invest in the program, and who needs training. Figure 10-4 illustrates a starting point example.

FUNCTION	DESCRIPTION	ACTIVITIES
IDENTIFY	Know the most critical assets	• Asset Management • Business Environment • Governance • Risk Assessment/ Strategy
PROTECT	Establish meaningful safeguards and behaviors around most critical information	• Access Control • Awareness and Training • Data Security • Information Protection • Maintenance • Protective Technology
DETECT	Monitor for and discover potential cybersecurity events	• Anomalies and Events • Continuous Monitoring • Detection Processes
RESPOND	Prepare for and mitigate cybersecurity events	• Response Planning • Communications (internal and external) • Analysis • Mitigation • Improvements (response)
RECOVER	Reduce the impact and maximize recovery time	• Recovery planning • Improvements (recovery) • Communications (internal and external)

Figure 10-4. *A simplified version of the CSF to get started*

The objective here is to become familiarized with the core functions for the CSF and what they mean to cybersecurity risk management and the associated activities that typically fit within each category. The functions are mutually exclusive. Building awareness of which organizational cybersecurity activity fits within which function helps set the foundation for the structure to work properly in covering a broad range of cybersecurity risks.

Following a known framework can also help address organizational needs, for example, structuring the organization (i.e., aligning staff and management). Using this framework can help provide a "quick win" for aligning resources to understand cybersecurity risks. Proper resource alignment is crucial to solving the risk problem (e.g., someone responsible for zero data loss, a lead for 100% uptime). Focusing attention on organizational structure based on authoritative sources helps decouple conflicting structures. The organizational operating structure will vary from organization to organization. The key is to have a clear information security risk owner (e.g., CISO, CRO, information security manager), where organizational incentives are established to maintain risk mitigation solutions. Figure 10-5 illustrates an example where the CISO organization is responsible for the program.

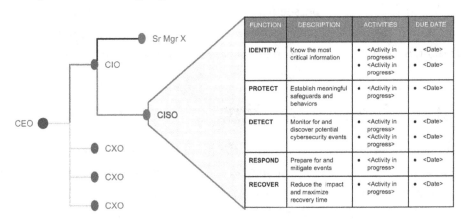

Figure 10-5. *Sample organizational structure with the cybersecurity risk program under the CISO*

With a well-defined, structured view of organizational cybersecurity risks, managing the risks as a program becomes possible. As the structure allows for planned activities, managers have a focal point to mitigate risks and track progress. However, at this point, the program structure is static—simply a documented set of foundational categories, with activities to address risks and due dates. The program needs action to become a bona fide action plan. This starts with a frequent review—a planned review of current progress toward the assigned due dates. This may seem like a clear and obvious point, but taking determined action to review the program is one that many organizations skip.

One major pitfall to avoid is over-indexing on one or two areas when managing a cybersecurity risk program. Many organizations begin and stay dedicated to managing activities that fall under Protect and Detect functions in the CSF. Naturally, these are the fun and challenging areas of cybersecurity. However, the Respond and Recover functions are the two key areas that focus attention on mitigating the cybersecurity risk *once the risk has become real.*

As an organization focused on reducing the impact of a cybersecurity event, be sure to spend time ensuring that the organization (as a whole) is ready to respond and recover in the event of a true cybersecurity incident.

Overall, a proper cybersecurity management program is structured to manage the broad aspects of security. When established, the program may contain output values in key areas that are used for decision support.

Then, Measure the Risk

Strategically placed measures within the program—and assigned to key cyber risk areas—help support tactical and strategic decisions (e.g., where to apply resources) in addressing the risk. In some cases, values from cyber risk measures act as a specific gauge for progress toward achieving a specified risk-acceptable goal: for example, reducing the number of out-of-date operating systems to zero across the entire organization.

In other cases, values from cyber risk measures act as a conjecture about possible risk-inducing activities that require investigation, for example, the number of employees demonstrating poor security behavior. In all cases, values from cybersecurity program measures need to provide insights to solve the overall risk problem.

What an organization chooses to measure in cybersecurity indicates the level at which they view the security problem. The objective is to quantify uncertainty in a way that provides decision-makers with the appropriate level of risk mitigation and coverage through measurement. Choosing insightful measures for managing risk, such as the time from vulnerability discovery to remediation, can indicate a tighter view on risk, which is more effective than simple informational facts, like the number of DDoS attacks over a certain period. And the sheer number of measures an organization uses at the organizational level indicates the maturity of the measures: that is, the ability for the total strategic measures to account for the appropriate measurement of risk.

The action of choosing an appropriate risk-informative set of measures may be broken down into key components for measuring this risk. These components may be the fundamentals for key performance indicators (KPIs), key risk indicators (KRIs), objectives and key results (OKRs), as well as simple measures. These measures may help management through feedback metrics. The following are some areas to measure and possible measures to apply:

- **Actionable management gaps** (e.g., time from discovered threat to response team activity)

- **Addressable activities** (e.g., number of employees demonstrating poor security behavior)

- **Insightful KPIs** (e.g., time to mitigate a critical threat, once detected)

- **Actionable reviews** (e.g., number of applications having security assessment)

- **Manageable risk areas** (e.g., number of third-party vendors with access to sensitive data and use of that data)

- **Actionable risk-reducing topics** (e.g., number of response plans tested under one year)

- **Correctable resource prioritization** (e.g., number of SLAs out of compliance due to an incident)

Management teams often struggle with both the actual math and the authoritative data sources to formulate a measure that provides an insightful value. Chances are that the data needed to feed the measure will not be readily available. Some find this a sticking point. However, a lack of data does not mean the measure is wrong; it just means the value cannot be calculated or derived immediately. When faced with the absence of either a clear equation or a required data source, avoid the tendency to drop the measure altogether for something easier. Instead, develop an interim measure to act as a surrogate to the harder measure until the data, or the equation, is available; because the data simply cannot be pulled from current sources is no reason to abandon a proper measure.

The critical objective is to choose risk-informative metrics, KRIs, and KPIs and then apply appropriate resources (e.g., measuring projects, overseeing initiatives) to act on the measures. Figure 10-6 highlights examples of proven measures.

FUNCTION	DESCRIPTION	...	MEASURE
IDENTIFY	Know the most critical assets	• ... • ... • ...	• % of assets identified as critical • % of employees passing annual Application Management Policy Awareness training • number of out-of-date systems operating
PROTECT	Establish meaningful safeguards and behaviors around most critical information	• ... • ... • ... • ... • ... • ... • ...	• % of privileged accounts are under privileged access control • % of Applications monitored for appropriate data quality use • number of employees demonstrating poor security behavior • Number of applications having security assessment • Mean time to patch (Date from when vuln comes out to when it is ACTUALLY patched) • number of business lines completing business-line application assessments • number of 3rd party vendors with access to sensitive data and use of that data
DETECT	Monitor for and discover potential cybersecurity events	• ...	• time from discovered threat to response team activity
RESPOND	Prepare for and mitigate cybersecurity events	• ...	• time to mitigate a critical threat, once detected
RECOVER	Reduce the impact and maximize recovery time	• ... • ...	• number of response plans tested under one year • number of SLA's out of compliance due to an incident

Figure 10-6. *Measures aligned to the CSF*

With some simple analysis, basic arithmetic is all that is needed to get started in measuring what works at the program level. But the main challenge is not the math. It is the data needed to provide the value. With agreement on what to measure, breaking down the properties to find the data needed to solve the measure becomes the next challenge, without sacrificing the math or the objective.

Providing a structured way to communicate, understand, and discuss cybersecurity is indispensable for consistency in reporting over time. Settling on a predetermined structure that is used every time for discussion provides a stable platform to address the various security elements relative to the observed change in risk. Not only is the content of the reporting consequential to decision-making, but the context is also vital to understanding where key risks exist. This is where strategic measures are taken into account.

Establishing a set of key measures presented in such a way that underpins the ability to measure progress and assign accountability supports the ability to make decisions while understanding the risk implications. The implementation of key risk measures should include the

top focus areas along the broad functions being measured for risk
(i.e., alongside the chosen framework) and no more than 15 measures to
start to maintain focus on the top risk areas.

Go Forth and Prosper

Laying down the foundational components of understanding, managing,
and measuring cybersecurity risks can help build an effective management
program. The program should eventually help solve organizational
management, technology, and executive oversight problems. Ideally, it
should reduce the business risks introduced by security weaknesses or
abuse of the underlying technology.

APPENDIX

Illustration

Solving cybersecurity risks within an organization begins with one approach. Enterprise cybersecurity risks continue to rise due to everything from advanced connectivity to the Internet of Things (IoT). They require more rapid response and persistent monitoring to appropriately identify and remediate vulnerabilities to protect enterprise assets. However, achieving overall enterprise cybersecurity is a multistep process that leaves many organizations uncertain about where to begin. This appendix takes the concepts from Chapter 5 and illustrates the step-by-step, structured, top-down approach as a first step in securing the enterprise.

Illustration: Structured Approach

To begin structuring a nascent cybersecurity program for management, take the following steps:

- **Step 1**. Set the structure.

- **Step 2**. Align risk-mitigating activities.

- **Step 3**. Assign roles and responsibilities.

- **Step 4**. Identify gaps, including third parties, and the appropriate activities to fill them.

- **Step 5**. Set the action plan (new for this appendix).

© Ryan Leirvik 2023
R. Leirvik, *Understand, Manage, and Measure Cyber Risk*,
https://doi.org/10.1007/978-1-4842-9319-5

Step 1. Set the Structure

To get started on a structured approach to addressing cybersecurity for your organization, begin with a known framework. The CSF is a good start, and a simplified version may be used. Figure A-1 is an example of a simplified version of the CSF used to get started.

FUNCTION	DESCRIPTION	ACTIVITIES
IDENTIFY	Know the most critical assets	• Asset Management • Business Environment • Governance • Risk Assessment/ Strategy • Supply Chain Risk Management
PROTECT	Establish meaningful safeguards and behaviors around most critical information	• Access Control • Awareness and Training • Data Security • Information Protection • Maintenance • Protective Technology
DETECT	Monitor for and discover potential cybersecurity events	• Anomalies and Events • Continuous Monitoring • Detection Processes
RESPOND	Prepare for and mitigate cybersecurity events	• Response Planning • Communications (internal and external) • Analysis • Mitigation • Improvements (response)
RECOVER	Reduce the impact and maximize recovery time	• Recovery planning • Improvements (recovery) • Communications (internal and external)

Figure A-1. *An example of a simplified version of the CSF used to get started*

With each function understood and properly described, align corresponding and appropriate risk-mitigating activities to each activity as part of a plan. Figure A-2 shows an example worksheet format, with the CSF activities retained as an outline to help ensure proper proposed activity coverage for each function. These are the activities proposed to address the risk in each category and complete the activities for each function, not the current activities already underway in the organization; that comes later.

FUNCTION	DESCRIPTION	ACTIVITIES	PROPOSED ACTIVITIES
IDENTIFY	Know the most critical assets	• Asset Management • Business Environment • Governance • Risk Assessment/ Strategy • Supply Chain Risk Management	• \<Proposed activity\> • \<Proposed activity\> • \<Proposed activity\> • \<Proposed activity\> • \<Proposed activity\>
PROTECT	Establish meaningful safeguards and behaviors around most critical information	• Access Control • Awareness and Training • Data Security • Information Protection • Maintenance • Protective Technology	• \<Proposed activity\> • \<Proposed activity\> • \<Proposed activity\> • \<Proposed activity\> • \<Proposed activity\>
DETECT	Monitor for and discover potential cybersecurity events	• Anomalies and Events • Continuous Monitoring • Detection Processes	• \<Proposed activity\> • \<Proposed activity\> • \<Proposed activity\>
RESPOND	Prepare for and mitigate cybersecurity events	• Response Planning • Communications (internal and external) • Analysis • Mitigation • Improvements (response)	• \<Proposed activity\> • \<Proposed activity\> • \<Proposed activity\> • \<Proposed activity\> • \<Proposed activity\>
RECOVER	Reduce the impact and maximize recovery time	• Recovery planning • Improvements (recovery) • Communications (internal and external)	• \<Proposed activity\> • \<Proposed activity\> • \<Proposed activity\>

Figure A-2. *Example worksheet format for mapping proposed activities*

With the mapping of proposed activities to recommended activities to address the spirit of the function, current cybersecurity activities (current activities) may be added.

Step 2. Align the Risk-Mitigating Activities

Assemble all the current cybersecurity-related initiatives, programs, or efforts (collectively referred to as *activities*). Each current activity or effort should fall into only one function and be aligned with only one recommended activity; recall that both functions and activities are mutually exclusive. Figure A-3 illustrates current activities using the worksheet format, where <Activity in progress> represents a current activity and <None> represents no current activity or a gap in the proposed-to-recommended activities.

FUNCTION	DESCRIPTION	ACTIVITIES	PROPOSED ACTIVITIES	CURRENT ACTIVITIES
IDENTIFY	Know the most critical assets	• Asset Management • Business Environment • Governance • Risk Assessment/ Strategy • Supply Chain Risk Management	• <Proposed activity> • <Proposed activity> • <Proposed activity> • <Proposed activity> • <Proposed activity>	• <Activity in progress> • <Activity in progress> • <Activity in progress> • <None> • <None>
PROTECT	Establish meaningful safeguards and behaviors around most critical information	• Access Control • Awareness and Training • Data Security • Information Protection • Maintenance • Protective Technology	• <Proposed activity> • <Proposed activity> • <Proposed activity> • <Proposed activity> • <Proposed activity> • <Proposed activity>	• <Activity in progress> • <Activity in progress> • <Activity in progress> • <None • <None • <None>
DETECT	Monitor for and discover potential cybersecurity events	• Anomalies and Events • Continuous Monitoring • Detection Processes	• <Proposed activity> • <Proposed activity> • <Proposed activity>	• <Activity in progress> • <None • <Activity in progress>
RESPOND	Prepare for and mitigate cybersecurity events	• Response Planning • Communications (internal and external) • Analysis • Mitigation • Improvements (response)	• <Proposed activity> • <Proposed activity> • <Proposed activity> • <Proposed activity> • <Proposed activity>	• <Activity in progress> • <None> • <Activity in progress> • <None> • <None>
RECOVER	Reduce the impact and maximize recovery time	• Recovery planning • Improvements (recovery) • Communications (internal and external)	• <Proposed activity> • <Proposed activity> • <Proposed activity>	• <Activity in progress> • <None> • <None>

Figure A-3. *Example worksheet format with the current activities*

With activities aligned to the appropriate function, a structured view into the organizational cybersecurity approach has emerged. This sets the foundation for managing the activities as a program.

Step 3. Assign Roles and Responsibilities

As with any good program management, individual responsibility is a key component of successfully managing cybersecurity. And one success factor to focus on here is the activity *lead*, that is, someone to take the lead on, and responsibility for, each risk mitigation initiative.

Responsibility for each respective activity will need to be assigned, and responsibility should be assigned by the title of the position (e.g., lead developer, head of physical security) over individual names to account for people changing positions and, therefore, cybersecurity responsibility. Figure A-4 provides a view of the worksheet expanded to capture responsibility for the listed activities.

FUNCTION	DESCRIPTION	ACTIVITIES	PROPOSED ACTIVITIES	CURRENT ACTIVITIES	RESPONSIBILITY
IDENTIFY	Know the most critical assets	• Asset Management • Business Environment • Governance • Risk Assessment/ Strategy • Supply Chain Risk Management	• <Proposed activity> • <Proposed activity> • <Proposed activity> • <Proposed activity> • <Proposed activity>	• <Activity in progress> • <Activity in progress> • <Activity in progress> • <None> • <None>	• <Title, Name> • <Title, Name> • <Title, Name> • <TBD> • <TBD>
PROTECT	Establish meaningful safeguards and behaviors around most critical information	• Access Control • Awareness and Training • Data Security • Information Protection • Maintenance • Protective Technology	• <Proposed activity> • <Proposed activity> • <Proposed activity> • <Proposed activity> • <Proposed activity> • <Proposed activity>	• <Activity in progress> • <Activity in progress> • <Activity in progress> • <None> • <None> • <None>	• <Title, Name> • <Title, Name> • <Title, Name> • <TBD> • <TBD> • <TBD>
DETECT	Monitor for and discover potential cybersecurity events	• Anomalies and Events • Continuous Monitoring • Detection Processes	• <Proposed activity> • <Proposed activity> • <Proposed activity>	• <Activity in progress> • <None> • <Activity in progress>	• <Title, Name> • <TBD> • <Title, Name>
RESPOND	Prepare for and mitigate cybersecurity events	• Response Planning • Communications (internal and external) • Analysis • Mitigation • Improvements (response)	• <Proposed activity> • <Proposed activity> • <Proposed activity> • <Proposed activity> • <Proposed activity>	• <Activity in progress> • <None> • <Activity in progress> • <None> • <None>	• <Title, Name> • <TBD> • <Title, Name> • <TBD> • <TBD>
RECOVER	Reduce the impact and maximize recovery time	• Recovery planning • Improvements (recovery) • Communications (internal and external)	• <Proposed activity> • <Proposed activity> • <Proposed activity>	• <Activity in progress> • <None> • <None>	• <Title, Name> • <TBD> • <TBD>

Figure A-4. *Worksheet expanded to capture responsibility for the listed activities*

Assigning roles is critical, especially with global or disparate teams. The organization's defensive posture can look good on paper, but a person must implement it and own its success (or failure). To aid success, assigning a due date for each activity helps track progress over time and offers a sense of planning for completing the activity and any program dependencies. Figure A-5 offers a view into a worksheet with activity due dates added.

FUNCTION	DESCRIPTION	ACTIVITIES	...	CURRENT ACTIVITIES	RESPONSIBILITY	DUE DATE
IDENTIFY	Know the most critical assets	• Asset Management • Business Environment • Governance • Risk Assessment/ Strategy • Supply Chain Risk Management	...	• \<Activity in progress\> • \<Activity in progress\> • \<Activity in progress\> • \<None\> • \<None\>	• \<Title, Name\> • \<Title, Name\> • \<Title, Name\> • \<TBD\> • \<TBD\>	• \<Date\> • \<Date\> • \<Date\> • \<N/A\> • \<N/A\>
PROTECT	Establish meaningful safeguards and behaviors around most critical information	• Access Control • Awareness and Training • Data Security • Information Protection • Maintenance • Protective Technology	...	• \<Activity in progress\> • \<Activity in progress\> • \<Activity in progress\> • \<None\> • \<None\> • \<None\>	• \<Title, Name\> • \<Title, Name\> • \<Title, Name\> • \<TBD\> • \<TBD\> • \<TBD\>	• \<Date\> • \<Date\> • \<Date\> • \<N/A\> • \<N/A\> • \<N/A\>
DETECT	Monitor for and discover potential cybersecurity events	• Anomalies and Events • Continuous Monitoring • Detection Processes	...	• \<Activity in progress\> • \<None\> • \<Activity in progress\>	• \<Title, Name\> • \<TBD\> • \<Title, Name\>	• \<Date\> • \<N/A\> • \<Date\>
RESPOND	Prepare for and mitigate cybersecurity events	• Response Planning • Communications (internal and external) • Analysis • Mitigation • Improvements (response)	...	• \<Activity in progress\> • \<None\> • \<Activity in progress\> • \<None\> • \<None\>	• \<Title, Name\> • \<TBD\> • \<Title, Name\> • \<TBD\> • \<TBD\>	• \<Date\> • \<N/A\> • \<Date\> • \<N/A\> • \<N/A\>
RECOVER	Reduce the impact and maximize recovery time	• Recovery planning • Improvements (recovery) • Communications (internal and external)	...	• \<Activity in progress\> • \<None\> • \<None\>	• \<Title, Name\> • \<TBD\> • \<TBD\>	• \<Date\> • \<N/A\> • \<N/A\>

Figure A-5. *Worksheet with activity due dates added*

Assigning titles and dates to initiatives has the added benefit of demonstrating resource constraints. Initiatives without assignments illustrate potential gaps in the security team. Titles with too many initiatives illustrate overloaded positions in the security team and a potential single point of failure should the person not be available for work suddenly (e.g., leave, fall ill, care for a family member). Overall, assigning roles ensures that the ownership and management of an activity are in place so that risk is not lost.

Step 4. Identify Gaps (Including Third Parties) and the Appropriate Activities to Fill Them

At this point, the gaps in program coverage are clear. This is the difference between the recommended activities and the current activities. Identifying these gaps provides a quick view of the possible weaknesses of the current cybersecurity program. Identifying these gaps and appropriate activities to fill them will offer future actions to take. Figure A-6 shows the highlighted program gaps, ready to be addressed.

FUNCTION	DESCRIPTION	ACTIVITIES	PROPOSED ACTIVITIES	CURRENT ACTIVITIES	RESPONSIBILITY
IDENTIFY	Know the most critical assets	• Asset Management • Business Environment • Governance • Risk Assessment/ Strategy • Supply Chain Risk Management	• <Proposed activity> • <Proposed activity> • <Proposed activity> • <Proposed activity> • <Proposed activity>	• <Activity in progress> • <Activity in progress> • <Activity in progress> • <None> • <None>	• <Title, Name> • <Title, Name> • <Title, Name> • <TBD> • <TBD>
PROTECT	Establish meaningful safeguards and behaviors around most critical information	• Access Control • Awareness and Training • Data Security • Information Protection • Maintenance • Protective Technology	• <Proposed activity> • <Proposed activity> • <Proposed activity> • <Proposed activity> • <Proposed activity> • <Proposed activity>	• <Activity in progress> • <Activity in progress> • <Activity in progress> • <None> • <None> • <None>	• <Title, Name> • <Title, Name> • <Title, Name> • <TBD> • <TBD> • <TBD>
DETECT	Monitor for and discover potential cybersecurity events	• Anomalies and Events • Continuous Monitoring • Detection Processes	• <Proposed activity> • <Proposed activity> • <Proposed activity>	• <Activity in progress> • <None> • <Activity in progress>	• <Title, Name> • <TBD> • <Title, Name>
RESPOND	Prepare for and mitigate cybersecurity events	• Response Planning • Communications (internal and external) • Analysis • Mitigation • Improvements (response)	• <Proposed activity> • <Proposed activity> • <Proposed activity> • <Proposed activity> • <Proposed activity>	• <Activity in progress> • <None> • <Activity in progress> • <None> • <None>	• <Title, Name> • <TBD> • <Title, Name> • <TBD> • <TBD>
RECOVER	Reduce the impact and maximize recovery time	• Recovery planning • Improvements (recovery) • Communications (internal and external)	• <Proposed activity> • <Proposed activity> • <Proposed activity>	• <Activity in progress> • <None> • <None>	• <Title, Name> • <TBD> • <TBD>

Figure A-6. Worksheet with highlighted program gaps in activities

With the gaps identified, new activities to satisfy the spirit of the recommended activities may be outlined and planned. This begins to set the road map for an action plan and, arguably, a long-term cybersecurity program.

One area to be mindful of during this step is the area of third-party risk. Anticipating areas of organizational cybersecurity risk does stretch beyond simply internal areas or domains. Individuals and entities outside of the organization (referred to as third parties) certainly introduce their own set of risks that can sometimes go overlooked. Take care to place security attention beyond the primary organizational boundaries for investigating possible vulnerabilities that may impact the primary organization.

Step 5. Set the Action Plan

A planned approach is ready to be set with a structured view of the cybersecurity risks and a set of activities to address them. Activities with assigned due dates in the near term may be communicated and tracked for progress. Activities with assigned due dates in the far term may be communicated, planned for, and established based on available resources. This simple approach becomes both an immediate action plan and a longer-term program plan to address key activities and plan available resources.

Once all the activities are planned with future completion dates, an agreement between relevant stakeholders can turn the action plan into a "road map" of initiatives, or activities, prioritized by risk for a practical cybersecurity program. Over time, a revisitation of the current corporate posture will help management maintain an active participant in reducing cybersecurity risks.

Index

A

Acceptable risk, 66
Actionable measures, 149, 150
Actionable reviews, 151, 152, 205
Actual risk management, 16, 28
Amass information, 58
Artificial intelligence
    continual good-*vs.*-evil use
        cases, 12
Asset categories, 48, 57
Asset class, 73, 76
Asset fundamentals, 50, 52
Asset inventory, 72, 73, 77, 78
Asset management, 45, 58, 76, 102
Asset management risk
    register, 200
Asset-relevant vulnerability
    information, 59
Assets, 23, 198, 199
Attack surface, 19

B

Board-level metrics, 179
Breach notification laws, 64
Business information security
    officer (BISO), 103

Business leaders, 13, 14
Business risk, 12
    management, 37
    problem, 37
Business's operations, 52, 175, 178

C

California Consumer
    Privacy Act, 65
California Privacy Rights Act, 65
Chasing perfection, 32
Chief information officer
    (CIO), 104
Chief information security officer
    (CISO), 70, 71, 75, 76,
        103, 203
Clarity, 52, 80, 182
Cloud services, 46, 102
Common Vulnerabilities and
    Exposures (CVE), 59
Common Vulnerability Scoring
    System (CVSS), 59
Computer hack, 22
Computer security, 64
Confidentiality, integrity, and
    availability (CIA), 23

© Ryan Leirvik 2023
R. Leirvik, *Understand, Manage, and Measure Cyber Risk*,
https://doi.org/10.1007/978-1-4842-9319-5

CPSIA information can be obtained
at www.ICGtesting.com
Printed in the USA
LVHW060014210623
750204LV00003B/193